cupcakes
and
cashmere

Editors: Rebecca Kaplan and Laura Dozier
Design: Topos Graphics
Production Manager: Kathy Lovisolo

Library of Congress Cataloging-in-
Publication Data

Schuman, Emily.
  Cupcakes and cashmere : a guide
for defining your style, reinventing
your space, and entertaining with ease /
by Emily Schuman.
    p. cm.
  ISBN 978-1-4197-0210-5 (hardback)
1. Fashion. 2. Entertaining.
3. Seasonal cooking. 4. Beauty,
Personal. I. Title.
  TT515.S38 2012
  746.9'2—dc23

       2012008030

Abrams books are available at special
discounts when purchased in quantity
for premiums and promotions as well as
fundraising or educational use. Special
editions can also be created to specification.
For details, contact specialsales@
abramsbooks.com or the address below.

ABRAMS
THE ART OF BOOKS SINCE 1949

115 West 18th Street
New York, NY 10011
www.abramsbooks.com

cupcakes
and
cashmere

a guide for defining your **STYLE**, reinventing your
SPACE, and **ENTERTAINING** with ease

emily schuman

Abrams Image, New York

contents

introduction

When I first began my blog, *Cupcakes and Cashmere*, in 2008, I wanted to create a place that brought together all the things I was passionate about. I was a few years out of college, and eager to find more of a balance, so that my life didn't revolve solely around my job.

After one particularly long week, I found myself bitter over seemingly trivial things—a parking ticket one day, a fight with my mom the next, and a dinner that came out looking more like a charred tire than a roast chicken. It occurred to me then that we all could use a reminder to focus on the little things that bring us happiness rather than dwelling on those that don't.

I started a recurring weekly post called "Five Things" that spoke to that exact idea. Unlike magazines that had one primary focus, I wanted to incorporate a variety of topics, including fashion, food, interior design, beauty, and entertaining. My goal was to create unique content on a daily basis that inspired others to live an elevated, charmed life.

This book revolves around the core ideas from my blog, but provides a much more in-depth view that simply can't be captured online. It's categorized by season, with my tips, tricks, and tutorials on how to make the most out of the different times of year. I share how to organize your closet as a part of spring cleaning, how to master beach beauty in summer, recipes that celebrate the flavors of fall, and a comprehensive winter gift guide. I hope you'll find this book full of inspirational ideas and helpful tips and tricks, and that it will serve as your go-to guide on how to celebrate life's little pleasures.

01.

spring

The year officially starts in January, but it always feels like spring is the time for new beginnings. Everything is fresh and vibrant, and I love the variety in the days—brisk mornings, warm afternoons, and chilly evenings. It's a time to get organized at home (I'm all about a good spring cleaning!), to pull out your pretty pastels that have been lying dormant all winter, and to slip into sandals without the addition of tights.

In this section, you'll find my favorite ways to embrace spring, an extensive guide on how to navigate flea markets, the five dresses every girl should have in her closet, how to organize jewelry in a way that's aesthetically pleasing, and ideas for how to spend the perfect spring day.

style

Springtime fashion should feel reinvigorated and fresh, full of colorful basics and classic staples that will bring your wardrobe to life. I'm always about simple dressing in spring and like to wear light layers, pretty chiffons, and bright prints.

spring closet checklist

1   Colorful skirt

2   Neutral satchel

3   Sleeveless blouse

4   Crisp shorts

5   Earth-tone sunglasses

6   Lightweight blazer

7   Cashmere cardigan

8   Bright headband/headscarf

9   Striped T-shirt

10 Trench coat

11 Vintage-inspired shift dress

12 Brown belt

13 Boyfriend jeans

14 Cropped trousers

15 Nude sandals

navigating flea markets

My obsession with flea markets began when I first moved to L.A. I was attempting to furnish my first place on a very tight budget and loved the idea of finding unique and affordable little treasures. One market in particular at Melrose and Fairfax, became a weekly ritual. I'd get up early in the morning, grab a cup of coffee, and head over to peruse each and every aisle. I found it therapeutic, exhilarating, and oftentimes very rewarding. Over the years, I've become quite the expert, so here are a few of my tips for navigating around a flea market.

what to wear

Dress in comfortable, casual clothes. Browsing through dusty old furniture and knickknacks is not an activity that calls for your wardrobe's best for two reasons: (1) you'll get dirty, and (2) if you're wearing something that looks expensive, you won't be able to bargain as efficiently. Be sure to wear layers if you plan on trying on clothes, and pack an extra pair of socks so you can test out shoes without going home with some sort of weird fungus. Bring sunglasses and a small bag you can wear on your shoulder or across your body.

come prepared

Before you go to the flea market, decide how much you want to spend. Since most vendors don't accept credit cards, pick up cash before you go. Limiting yourself to this amount is a great way to stick to your budget. If you're looking for furniture or art, know the dimensions of your place. There's nothing worse than coming home with a perfect sofa that's too big to fit in your living room. Have an idea of things you need (vases, bookends, jewelry), so you're on the lookout, but also be open to discovering random pieces that you hadn't considered before.

strike a deal

Knowing how to bargain at a flea market is one of the most crucial parts of the experience. Here's how to go about getting something for the price you want:

1 Once you've found something you love, ask yourself how much you'd be willing to pay.

2 From there, you can either ask for the price you want ("Would you take twenty dollars for this?") or simply ask, "What's the lowest price you'd take for this?" Either way, you'll get a good idea of how much the vendor wants. I typically ask the latter, just in case he or she is willing to sell it for a lot less than what I had imagined paying.

3 If the vendor asks for more than your ideal price, start the bargaining process. Ask for a price lower than your target amount so that you can meet in the middle.

4 If the seller isn't willing to budge, take out cash. Often, if you have it in your hands and offer it one last time, a vendor will just go for the quick sale.

5 If you're unable to come to an agreement on the price, walk away. Think about it for a while, and if you truly can't go home without it, buy it. Chances are, you won't regret it.

examine items carefully

While buying antique or vintage items is part of the main appeal of shopping at a flea market, their age can also be one of the biggest annoyances. It's important to thoroughly inspect items before you bring them home. If there are flaws, make sure they can be fixed.

clothing
Look for rips, tears along seams, missing buttons, broken zippers, discolorations, and stains. I've come home far too many times with a great item, only to discover a gaping hole that's not fixable. The same goes for shoes: make sure to examine the outer material and the sole, and see how they hold up when you walk around in them for a bit.

furniture
Make sure things are well constructed and sturdy, and consider whether they could possibly be reupholstered, dyed, or painted.

things to look for

clothing
When it comes to clothes, I try to search for things that aren't readily available in stores. Look for special detailing that sets an item apart—whether it's an intricate collar, a pretty pattern, or an interesting cut. Always remember that things can be tailored, as long as they're not too small, so if you fall in love with the pleating on a skirt that's a tad too long or a preppy blazer that's still rocking big shoulder pads those are easy fixes for a professional.

Specifically: blazers (usually those made for boys), '70s sundresses (for more on dress shopping at flea markets, see Finding the Perfect Vintage Sundress, page 55), sequined tops, and vintage Levi's cutoffs.

accessories
Among the easiest things to acquire at a flea market (even for a beginner) are accessories. It's not hard to find something that fits, and accessories are a great way to incorporate vintage pieces into a more current wardrobe.

Specifically: sunglasses (look for varying shapes, sizes, colors, and any special details), belts, boots, clutches (look for unexpected materials and sizes—either really big or small), and silk scarves (tie one on a bag, wear it in your hair, or use it in lieu of a belt).

home
Nearly all the most treasured items in my home are from flea markets. See the following pages for a few examples of some of my favorite finds. Their age adds such character and acts as a nice complement to modern furnishings.

Specifically: mirrors, trays, buckets, baskets, art, chairs, and kitchen supplies (cake stands, bowls, cups, and vases).

soles of spring

One of my favorite changes that comes with spring is the transition from tights and boots to sandals and bare feet. Though certain trends come and go (case in point: gladiators), there are a few shoes that I rely on, wear after year.

1

Nude platforms.
Perfect for day or night, they are elongating and light and fresh for spring.

2

Wooden wedges.
These are a great way to add a natural element to your ensemble and to balance out girly apparel. I like them to have at least a one-inch platform.

3

Short ankle boots.
These boots are great for those chilly days when you don't want to wear a high boot and also are cute with sweater dresses and cuffed jeans.

4

Patent sandals.
Transitional, but slightly dressier sandals than leather, these are perfect for brunch or with a maxi dress at night.

5

Bright pumps.
A classic pump in a fun color is ideal for adding a bit of life to a neutral outfit.

layering jewelry

I'm a big fan of layering jewelry, as it provides a great starting point for the rest of your ensemble. I almost always have a stack of bracelets on one arm that looks relatively thrown-together but is actually quite planned. The trick when layering jewelry, whether necklaces, bracelets, or rings, is to have the selection look unforced but cohesive. Here are some of the ways I mix and match different accessories.

bracelets

Start with one main focal point. Whether it's a chunky bracelet or a colorful bangle, let it be the jumping-off place for the rest of the pieces. Then build from there, trying to make the look intentional, but not too matchy-matchy. Don't worry about mixing metals (I love the combination of yellow gold with rose gold), and look to incorporate different textures and shapes. The end result should be an interesting combination that looks chic and eye-catching.

rings

When it comes to rings, balance is key. So if you're wearing a large cocktail ring on one hand, stick to smaller rings on the other. My favorite way to wear rings is to stack them on one finger, with a few plain delicate bands mixed in with different gemstones.

necklaces

Necklaces are best when they're a variety of lengths, with the shortest falling to the clavicle and the longest hitting mid-sternum. A creative combination of necklaces adds great texture to whatever you're wearing and even looks good tucked into a blouse or dress.

brooches and pins

I like wearing vintage brooches in groups, since I find it makes them feel more modern. I go for common shapes that are easy to find in multiples (like rhinestones in circles or bows) and then wear them as a cluster on a blazer pocket or lapel.

a dress for multiple occasions

I always had an entire section dedicated to dresses in my closet, but when I used to need one for a specific occasion, I never felt like I was adequately prepared. I've since implemented more of a system, organizing my dresses by type, and have compiled a list of the five dresses that every girl should have in her closet.

1 **bright shift dress**
Shift dresses are nice for daytime occasions, whether a graduation or a bridal shower. Wear it with heels, since this style can look a bit matronly with flats or sandals.

2 **professional dress**
Find a dress that strikes the balance of being not too revealing but still flattering. I like neutral colors or subtle patterns that you can wear a variety of ways. It should look great dressed up (with a trench coat and heels) or more casual (with patent-leather ballet flats and a sweater).

3 **lbd**
The little black dress is provocative, yet demure. It should be able to take you from the office to a fancy cocktail hour. This is one item I'd recommend saving up for, since it will probably be the most versatile item you own (note: if you can't spend a lot on the dress, at least take it to a good tailor so that the fit is close to perfect). Make sure it's a classic shape and is a flattering cut for your body.

4 **sequins**
The obligatory New Year's Eve/Vegas/perfect party dress—it should make you feel amazing every time you throw it on. Look for fun details like an open back or slits on the arms. If you're going to go short, make sure it has a modest top (my favorite is a long-sleeved mini dress), and the same goes for if it's low cut: make sure that it doesn't hit too high above the knee. Pair it with a nude or black heel, so you don't distract from the dress.

5 **sweater dress**
Make sure it's not too short, which can make people suspect you are wearing a regular sweater without pants. This dress should be cozy and cute, perfect for running errands on a chilly afternoon. Whether you wear it with tights and heels or barelegged with ankle booties, it's a great piece that looks polished but effortless.

beauty

Spring beauty should be
pared down, simple, and pretty.
Think glowy skin, pink lips,
and natural hair.

5 spring beauty must-haves for any budget

1 **Hair:** deep conditioner (necessary after months of dry, cold weather). *Splurge*: Kérastase. *Steal*: Neutrogena's "Triple Moisture."

2 **Face:** bronzer (an easy way to look like you've gotten just a smidge of springtime sun on your cheeks). *Splurge*: Nars's "Laguna." *Steal*: Wet n Wild's "Mego Glo Illuminating Powder."

3 **Body:** light floral fragrance (great for layering—I love orange blossom, gardenia, and jasmine). *Splurge*: Annick Goutal's "Petite Cherie." *Steal*: Juicy Couture's "Viva La Juicy."

4 **Lips:** a light pink lipstick (brightens your face without looking too "done"). *Splurge*: MAC's "Snob." *Steal*: Revlon's "Pink Part."

5 **Nails:** pretty pastels in different shades (to mix and match on your hands and feet). *Splurge*: Chanel's "Coco Blue." *Steal*: Essie's "Borrowed Blue."

* All Splurge items are shown on the left, Steal items on the right.

how to: glowy skin

The secret behind getting a glowy look is starting with very moisturized skin. Even before you put on makeup, it should have a nice sheen that will only be improved with a bit of coverage. Here are my techniques for looking luminescent.

tools

Moisturizer
Tinted moisturizer
Illuminating gel
Concealer
Bronzer
Highlighting powder
Cheek stain
Eyelash curler
Mascara

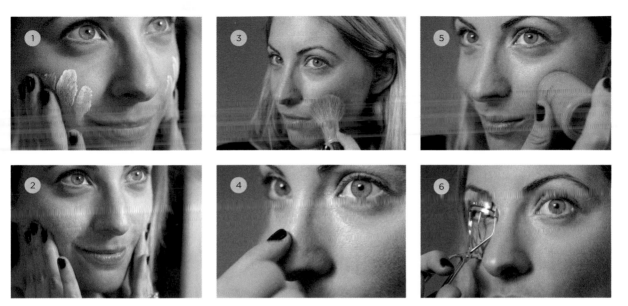

1 Moisturize your skin with a lotion that has both SPF and some sort of reflective qualities (I like Aveeno's Positively Radiant line). In your hand, mix two parts tinted moisturizer (I like Laura Mercier) with one part illuminating gel (Nars makes a great one, as does Revlon) and apply this all over your face and neck. Blend well.

2 Add concealer only where necessary (I use one by Time Balm)—on blemishes or around your eyes or nose.

3 Lightly swipe bronzer (Nars's "Laguna" is my favorite) across your forehead, down the bridge of your nose, along your cheekbones, and on your chin. Just remember to use a light hand, so the color is added gradually and looks natural.

4 Apply highlighting powder along your brow bone and down the bridge of your nose. (MAC makes a great highlighting powder, but you can also use pearly white eye shadow for this—I use one by Neutrogena.)

5 Rub a cheek stain onto the apples of your cheeks (try Benefit's "Benetint" or Tarte's "Dollface").

6 Curl your eyelashes (nothing beats Shu Uemura's version of this tool) and add a coat of black mascara (Maybelline's "Lash Stiletto" goes on clump-free).

how to: blow-dry hair

While most people have naturally wavy, curly, or straight hair, I would categorize mine as frizzy and unruly. It also happens to be color-treated and incredibly thick, which makes blow-drying it a royal pain. Thankfully, I've picked up tons of tricks over the years so that I'm now able to give myself a blow-out that rivals those at the salon. It takes a bit of time to master (especially getting over the intimidation factor of using a round brush), but here are my steps to getting hair that's smooth and sleek, with a natural bounce.

tools

Hair towel
  (it speeds up the
  drying time)
Round brush
Styling cream
Blow-dryer
Hair ties
Hair clips
Hair spray

1 After shampooing and conditioning, wrap your hair tightly in a towel and secure it on top of your head for at least 10 minutes so your hair won't be sopping wet when you begin.

2 Remove the towel and brush your hair so it's tangle-free.

3 Apply product (I like to use styling creams that also tackle frizz like Moroccan Oil or Bumble and bumble's "Grooming Creme").

4 With the blow-dryer on the hottest setting, start to dry your hair, concentrating on the roots and running your fingers through to separate strands.

5 For extra volume, use a round brush to lift hair at the roots. At this stage you want your hair to be about 80 percent dry.

6 Divide your hair into three sections, and secure the bottom two with rubber bands. Begin with the very top section and, using your round brush, create tension by pulling hair taut, and direct air at the root of the hair, then slowly move out toward the ends.

7 Once the top section is dry, use a clip to secure it on top of your head. Follow the same steps for the two bottom sections of hair.

8 After all three sections of hair have been dried, remove the clips and lightly spray some hair spray over your entire head to help control flyaways.

at home

It's nice to lighten up your place after winter, freeing it from heavy blankets and dark colors, and one of the things I most look forward to is spring cleaning. Though it's a lot of work, the results are so rewarding and it's a great way to embrace the new season.

office organization— the tipping point

I'm organizationally challenged, and up until recently, my place had absolutely no order or structure. I didn't own a filing cabinet (let alone a single file), my drawers were bursting with odds and ends, and most of my things didn't have a designated place. This all changed when I made it a priority to create a system that not only kept things organized, but also was aesthetically pleasing.

I realized that my teetering stacks of papers, receipts, and documents had to go, so I bought a simple filing cabinet (from CB2) and started organizing. The hardest part is implementing a system that works, but once it's been created, your life will be free of clutter and chaos.

categorize
Pick several main categories that will work for you. Mine are Home, Legal, Personal, Financial, Medical, Blog, and To Do. I keep a small filing folder on my desk that has these main sections divided out, so when I'm in a rush and don't have time to file things completely, I just stick papers into their corresponding category.

create subsections
In my filing cabinet, I have my main categories (listed above), with smaller folders within each that are more specific. For example, within my Financial section, I have folders dedicated to things like Banking, Taxes, Bills, Social Security, etc.

give everything a place
Think beyond the obvious sections and include things that are typically left uncategorized. If you want a secure place to store your passport, a folder that keeps track of gift ideas, or a file dedicated to your pets, create one.

get professional
Instead of messily scribbling down each section within your filing system, purchase a label maker. It's a great investment that will help keep your folders looking clean and concise, and can also be used in numerous other ways (for labeling jars in the kitchen or bathroom essentials, for example).

go digital

Almost everything these days can be created or stored electronically, so consider a digital filing system. It's environmentally sound and creates much less clutter. Make sure all statements are sent to you via e-mail instead of snail mail; important documents, photographs, or other valuable papers can be scanned and saved on your computer. The most critical aspect of storing things electronically is to be vigilant about backing up your work. I set a reminder for myself once a month to transfer my work from my computer onto an external hard drive that I keep in my filing cabinet for easy access.

separate

To ensure your desk drawers stay neat, measure out the space and buy dividers so that all of your office supplies are easily accessible.

jeweled corners

I'm a firm believer that jewelry should not be stowed away in drawers to collect dust. Instead, display it. It will be a part of your home's decor, and simultaneously will remind you to wear what you own.

necklaces
I used to keep all my necklaces together in a drawer, but lost patience with constantly having to detangle them. I now keep them on a vintage mannequin bust that helps brighten up the room and also makes accessorizing that much simpler.

rings/bracelets/brooches
I keep all my rings, bracelets, and brooches in simple vintage dishes. They're easy to see (so I use them more often), and I love how the antique feel of the saucers makes them part of my room's decor.

closet clutter—
clothes uncovered

One of the best things about having a functional closet is that you can actually see everything you own and are much more likely to wear it. When things are hidden and crammed into corners, your wardrobe never feels complete, and getting dressed becomes a hassle.

edit

Make sure your closet is filled only with items that are flattering, comfortable, and on trend. There's no use holding on to things that you never wear. This creates clutter and prohibits you from having a well-rounded wardrobe. It doesn't matter if something was a gift or you're keeping it for sentimental reasons; if you're not reaching for it on a regular basis (at least a couple of times a year), donate it.

take inventory

If you already have three pairs of skinny jeans and a collection of black blazers, downsize. Keep only the ones you love, that are in good condition, fit perfectly, and are still current.

utilize space

Whether you have a large walk-in or a miniature closet that would be better equipped to hold doll clothes, make the most of it. Invest in slimline hangers that take up less space, use pretty boxes to store things like scarves and gloves, and buy shelf dividers so that you can line up all your bags without them getting squished or falling over each time you remove one.

make it pretty

The best dressing rooms in stores always have great details, which makes trying on clothes a much more enjoyable experience. Bring those elements into your own home by making small changes that have a big impact. Make sure all your hangers are the same size and color, keep things well lit (with flattering light!), keep an unlit candle nearby to make things smell nice, and consider lining your shelves or walls with wallpaper.

focus on what you wear most

Organize your closet based on what you will be reaching for most often. Since I'm frequently in dresses or skirts and tops, I make sure they're easy to access and clearly visible. On the other hand, since I don't wear jeans too often, I fold them neatly on a shelf that's not as centrally located.

know what you need

When you have an organized closet and a good idea of what you own, it also can help point out things that are missing, which can help you determine what items you should buy in order to create a well-rounded wardrobe. For instance, you might realize that you have a lot of mini skirts, but none that are longer or professional (like a pencil skirt).

keep track of what you're looking for

If you already have plenty of skirts or blouses in your closet, take note of what you're missing (like trousers or a black blazer). It will make your shopping trips much more focused, and you'll come home with things you actually need, instead of adding bulk to your closet. I keep a running list on my computer and add to it whenever I think of a key piece I'm missing or simply admire something while browsing through magazines.

food and entertaining

Spring is one of the best times to take advantage of fresh produce. Farmers' markets are bursting with colorful fruits and vegetables, warm weather is on the horizon, and it's an ideal time to experiment in the kitchen.

bloody mary brunch bar

I first fell in love with Bloody Marys during a trip to New Orleans. They're an integral part of the brunch culture there, and I've since ditched my old favorite brunch beverage (mimosas) in lieu of the spicy drink. Paired with simple, savory foods (I prefer homemade egg sandwiches), a Bloody Mary bar is a great way to kick off a lazy weekend morning.

In order to create a great Bloody Mary bar, you should stock up on lots of different accoutrements that people can use to dress up their drinks (the list on the next page provides plenty of suggestions). Since I like the idea of being able to completely customize your own drink, I serve tomato juice instead of a Bloody Mary mix. It allows people to adjust the salt and spice levels to their own liking, but there's nothing wrong with starting with a premade option. For a festive touch, you can rim the glasses in a spicy/salt mixture.

setting the mood

Brunch should be a relaxed meal—a leisurely time for friends to catch up over great food and drinks. Since you don't want to be in the kitchen while everyone's over, try to prepare things that can be whipped together beforehand. Bloody Marys are a spicy, savory drink, so they should be paired with simple comfort food.

what to serve

My favorite things to serve are egg sandwiches. They're easy, everyone likes them, and they're simple to make in big batches. Set your oven to about 250°F, arrange English muffins or ciabatta rolls faceup on a baking sheet, and bake them for a few minutes to brown them slightly. While they're in the oven, prepare your fried eggs (one per sandwich), salt lightly, and add chopped chives at the end. At this point, you can add a slice of cheese or bacon before assembling the sandwich.

Also provide spiced nuts and pretzels or bagel chips in pretty bowls for snacking.

tools

Tomato juice
  (I buy a low-sodium version, so people can control
  how salty their drink is)
Alcohol
  (vodka is typical, but I like to have gin on hand too,
  for those who prefer it)
Lime wedges and lemon wedges
Kosher salt and celery salt
Tabasco and Worcestershire sauce
Prepared horseradish
Angostura bitters
Cayenne pepper and black pepper
Chopped shallots
Celery stalks
Olives
  (and some sort of cocktail pick or toothpick)
Pickled carrots/okra/onions/green beans
Ice
  (I freeze tomato juice in ice cube trays the night
  before, so people's drinks don't get watered down)
Tall glasses
Coarse sea salt and chili powder
  (to rim the glasses)

my ideal bloody mary

In a mixing glass, add 4 oz low-sodium tomato
juice, 2 oz vodka, 4 dashes of Tabasco, 3 dashes
of Worcestershire sauce, ½ teaspoon prepared
horseradish, 1 dash of Angostura bitters, ½ teaspoon
celery salt, and the juice of 1 lime. Stir together then
add tomato ice cubes and a celery stalk.

20 ideas for how to spend a spring day

1   Gather up sports equipment to bring to the park (badminton, Smashball, croquet, cornhole, bocce).

2   Bring a stack of magazines to read at a coffee shop.

3   Reorganize your closet and donate clothes to charity (see page 32).

4   After completing item 3, take yourself shopping for something new.

5   Indulge in spa-inspired activities, such as a long bath, DIY mani/pedis, face masks, etc.

6   Make a picnic to enjoy at a concert.

7   Buy fresh fruit and blend it up to make homemade Popsicles.

8   Visit a local thrift shop or flea market (see page 13).

9   Create your own stationery from plain envelopes and cards, stamps, watercolors, and any extra fabric you have lying around (lace makes a really pretty edge on a card).

10 Make old items around the house new again with a fresh coat of (bright) paint.

11 Take a jewelry-making class with a friend.

12 Challenge yourself in the kitchen by cooking something you've never made before with fresh spring ingredients.

13 On a rainy day, host a movie-watching pajama party featuring classic films and popcorn.

14 Buy or rent a good SLR camera and spend the entire day taking pictures.

15 Dye old clothing fun new colors.

16 Look up reviews for restaurants and try one you've never been to.

17 Host a classic brunch, complete with mimosas, eggs Benedict, and waffles with fresh fruit.

18 Find a TV series to watch on DVD and host a marathon (or watch by yourself).

19 Re-cover books with beautiful paper.

20 Take a floral arranging class. Then buy flowers and start making bouquets (see Fawning over Flora, page 42).

entertaining essentials

I was a nervous wreck the first time I ever hosted a dinner party at my place. My studio at the time hardly fit my bed and a small sofa, so entertaining was a bit of a challenge. The thing I quickly realized, though, was that it took only a few things to make my place party-ready, despite its size. Don't stress if your place isn't perfect or large enough to accommodate a group (for my first dinner, we sat on pillows around my coffee table). Instead, focus on the key elements to make sure everyone has an enjoyable time.

hosting arsenal

Here are the main things to have on hand (besides dinner and dessert) when hosting at your place.

1 **Appetizers:** crackers, cheese, olives, cornichons, and a baguette

2 **Drinks:** a bottle of chilled champagne, flat or still water, and some sort of soda

3 **Accessories:** cocktail napkins, toothpicks, and ice

rule to live by

Keep your place ten minutes away from being guest ready. My house isn't always spotless but it's neat enough so that I can throw dirty laundry in the hamper, clear the dishes from the sink, and straighten up the living room so that I can play hostess in a matter of minutes.

tools

Candles (keep them unscented, unless in the bathroom)
Vases (filled with fresh flowers)
Trays (a pretty place to keep little knickknacks such as figurines, candles, and books)
Serving platter/bowl
Stemware (think outside the box and use Mason jars instead of champagne flutes)
Utensils
Bowls and plates (two different sizes)
Napkins
Places to sit (can be chairs, sofa, or pillows on the floor)
Music

fawning over flora— creating a beautiful bouquet

I love having fresh flowers in my place. It's the quickest way to bring a room to life and a fun way to incorporate different color palettes without making a long-term commitment. But the work begins before you even head to the store. First, there is the question of theme. Are you going for one specific color (like all white or sunshine yellow)? Are you looking for tall flowers? A mix-and-match variety that resembles wildflowers? You don't have to actually commit to anything ahead of time; just keep your ideas in mind as you evaluate what looks freshest at the market and what will create a cohesive bouquet.

I avoid buying premixed bouquets since I like to choose which flowers will be included (plus they often tend to look a bit cheap). That being said, I do like having several different kinds of flowers bunched together, since it keeps things looking interesting and adds depth. Search for different sizes, textures, and colors that complement each other. Buy the flowers in odd numbers (like five roses or three calla lilies)—this creates a good balance within your bouquet.

I definitely have favorite flowers I gravitate toward (here I used white carnations, scabiosas, roses, and Casablanca lilies), but the problem I always had was how to make them look good once I got them home. I invited my friend Rachel over to share some of her tips for making the perfect floral arrangement.

tools

Flowers of your choice
Kitchen shears or scissors
Wire
Flower frog
  (not necessary, but
  extremely helpful)
Ribbon or raffia
  (optional)

1 Arrange flowers by type. It's easier to know how to distribute flowers evenly when you work with one kind at a time. Once you've arranged the flowers into separate categories, prune them by using the scissors to snip off any leaves (they just make the arrangement look messy).

2 Use a flower frog. I had no idea what these were until Rachel told me about them, but I now consider them necessities. They resemble miniature combs that

you place on the bottom of a vase and then use to stabilize stems. It helps keep the shape of your arrangement so that flowers don't simply droop over the sides.

3 Start big. Create a focal point to your bouquet with your most prominent flowers.

4 Add on. Arrange your biggest flowers so they are nicely balanced and then build around that. Once you have constructed the arrangement around the central flowers, trim the stems. Keep them longer than you think you need and cut accordingly from there (it's better to do it that way than to accidentally cut them too short).

5 When all flowers are in place, make sure that all sides look even. Also, don't forget the finishing touches. Add water and a final detail like wrapping a ribbon or some raffia around the vase.

flowers on a budget

You don't have to spend a lot in order to have beautiful, fresh flowers around the house. Think beyond elaborate bouquets and instead purchase one type of flower (like miniature roses, which typically sell for under ten dollars a dozen). When bunched together in a tight, compact bouquet and put in a small vase, the effect will be chic and stylish.

perfecting playlists

I'm a huge proponent of playing good music when you have company. It's the easiest way to set the right atmosphere and can help determine the pace, no matter what the occasion.

First, consider the event and decide what kind of vibe you want to achieve. Is it a midmorning brunch with your most energetic friends? A low-key dinner on a Thursday night? This will help establish the type of music to play.

Next, make sure there is a beginning, middle, and end. It will help create a good flow and will ensure the same type of music isn't playing for the duration of your event. Lastly, include a good mix of artists—some contemporary mixed with classics, as it makes for a diverse and varied listening experience.

three parts to a playlist

1 Upbeat—Play familiar songs that have good energy to welcome your arriving guests.

2 Mellow and steady—This should make up the majority of the playlist. Choose songs that will never dominate the conversation.

3 Calm and slow—At this stage, the music can help to signify that the party is coming to an end.

grilled shrimp and asparagus salad

I've never been one of those girls who found just any salad satisfying. They'd keep me full momentarily, but for the most part, they were boring and bland. That all changed the moment I started adding grilled vegetables and shrimp (which can easily be swapped for another form of protein, if you prefer). This is easy to whip up and packed full of flavor—the ideal spring salad.

ingredients

Serves 2

salad

- 1 pound (16- to 18-count) shrimp, peeled and deveined
- 4 tablespoons olive oil
- 1 teaspoon salt
- Freshly ground pepper
- 1 bunch asparagus
- 1 tablespoon fresh lemon juice
- 1 Hass avocado
- 1 ripe mango
- 2 tomatoes
- 2 Persian cucumbers
- ½ cup roughly chopped cilantro

dressing

- ¼ cup freshly squeezed lemon juice
- 1 tablespoon chopped shallots
- 1 tablespoon Dijon mustard
- 1 teaspoon honey
- ½ teaspoon salt
- ¼ teaspoon freshly ground pepper
- ½ cup extra-virgin olive oil
- 1 tablespoon sesame seeds

1 Preheat the oven to 400°F. Place the shrimp on a sheet pan and drizzle them with 2 tablespoons of the olive oil, ½ teaspoon of the salt, and a pinch of pepper. Toss to combine and spread them out in a single layer on the pan. Roast the shrimp for 6 minutes, or until they are pink and firm to the touch.

2 Chop the asparagus into 3-inch pieces, discarding the tough bottom part of the stalks. In a separate sheet pan, drizzle the asparagus with the remaining 2 tablespoons of olive oil and ½ teaspoon of salt; add the lemon juice and a pinch of pepper. Toss to combine and then spread the pieces out in a single layer on the pan. Roast the asparagus for 8 to 10 minutes, until the pieces soften slightly.

3 Place the shrimp and asparagus in a large serving bowl and set the mixture aside until it comes to room temperature. Dice the avocado, mango, tomatoes, and cucumbers and add them to the bowl. Add the chopped cilantro and gently mix it all together.

4 For the dressing, whisk the lemon juice, shallots, mustard, honey, salt, and pepper in a small bowl. Shortly before serving, slowly beat in the olive oil until the vinaigrette is emulsified, pour the dressing over the salad, and toss gently. Sprinkle sesame seeds over the top.

basic vinaigrette

ingredients

Makes enough for a salad to serve 2

- 1 teaspoon minced shallots
- ½ teaspoon Dijon mustard
- 2 tablespoons fresh lemon juice
- ½ teaspoon salt
- ¼ teaspoon freshly ground pepper
- 4 tablespoons extra-virgin olive oil

I haven't bought a bottled salad dressing in years. Simple vinaigrettes take so little time to whip together that it really doesn't make sense to choose something prepackaged. Adapting the dressing for the Grilled Shrimp and Asparagus Salad by removing the honey and sesame seeds, for instance, creates a more basic recipe that lends itself to a wide variety of salads. Create your own versatile dressing at home with this foolproof recipe.

In a bowl, combine the shallots with the mustard. Stir in the lemon juice, then add salt and pepper. Very gradually pour in the olive oil while whisking it all together; this will create an emulsion. Pour the dressing over your favorite greens and serve immediately.

spring cocktail: mint julep

This classic cocktail, featuring plenty of mint, is as refreshing as it is vibrant. It looks best when served in a julep cup (I pick them up anytime I spot them at a flea market), but is appealing in a plain tall glass too.

ingredients

Makes 1 cocktail

- 20 fresh mint leaves, plus 1 mint sprig for garnish
- 2 teaspoons sugar
- 1 teaspoon water
- Crushed ice
- 2 ounces bourbon

In a julep cup or tall glass, muddle the mint leaves with the sugar and water until the sugar is dissolved. Add crushed ice to the glass, then pour in bourbon and stir briskly. Finish with the mint sprig.

Tipsy Tip: I fill up ice cube trays with water, add a fresh sprig of mint to each square, and pop the trays in the freezer. It's a great way to dress up any drink and add a bit of color.

02.

summer

I've been out of school for quite some time, but I still get that same sense of childish excitement at the onset of summer. When I was in high school, my friends and I had a recurring date on the first day of summer break. We'd pile into the car and head out onto the curvy road that led to Stinson Beach. Of course in northern California, it doesn't actually get warm until well into August, so we would sit bundled in sweatshirts with our feet in the sand.

In order to help you take advantage of the long days and warm nights, I've compiled some of my favorite things about summer. You'll find delicious, easy-to-make recipes, beauty tips for hot weather, and how to create a balanced wardrobe of casual and polished pieces.

style

Due to the heat, summer fashion should
be simple and comfortable. I drift toward
fuss-free essentials in neutral colors that
look crisp and clean.

summer closet checklist

1. Cream/white/nude-colored blazer

2. Kimono-style robe/dress/kaftan

3. Skinny belt

4. Versatile daytime dress (perfect for a day at the beach or a casual get-together)

5. A pair of shorts for your body type (cutoffs, high-waisted, or relaxed and loose)

6. Gold dainty jewelry

7. A wrinkle-resistant blouse (preferably made of cotton or linen)

8. Cotton pants

9. Bright clutch

10. Retro-inspired swimsuit (for lounging poolside at swanky hotels)

11. Light denim

12. Straw hat

13. Striped cardigan

14. Flowy skirt

15. Flat sandals

rules of fashion

When I first became interested in fashion toward the end of high school, I was meticulous about adhering to certain rules. I was careful never to mix pieces from different seasons (a summer skirt with a heavy sweater or open-toed sandals in cold weather), I never wore contrasting patterns, was adamant about steering clear of tapered jeans, and made sure not to wear white before Memorial Day. Those types of rules now seem stiff and restrictive, and I break them on what seems to be a daily basis (I love a good leopard print mixed with stripes). Now I rely on several loose guidelines of sorts, but follow the philosophy that nothing is ever truly off-limits.

- **Wear what makes you happy, confident, and comfortable.**

- **Don't wear more than two trends at once** (see Trendy Behavior, page 92).

- **Know your strengths** (and accentuate them). If you have long legs, a small waist, or delicate wrists, wear things that highlight these features, and remember what works. Think A-line skirts, waist-cinching dresses, or three-quarter-length sleeves.

- **Be aware of your weaknesses** (and divert attention accordingly). If you have a great bust, but a doughy middle, opt for tops with a little give around the stomach and that play up your shoulders or clavicle.

- **Get out of your comfort zone every once in a while.** I primarily live in dresses and skirts, solid colors, and neutral heels, but when I switch things up a bit (by wearing tight pants, a patterned top, and bright platforms), it's refreshing and makes me feel like I'm playing dress-up.

finding the perfect vintage sundress

There are certain things that are always on my list whenever I go to a flea market, and a vintage sundress is one of them. You can never have enough little dresses that are packed with interesting details, and they are among the easiest things you can throw on. Here are my tips for how to spot the perfect one.

1   **Pay attention to shape.** If you look good in boatneck tops, dresses with a cinched waist, or about the knee skirts, these are the features you should be looking for. If it's a little big/billowy/long, that's okay; you can always get it altered later.

2   **Seek out details.** One of the biggest advantages to buying vintage clothing is the attention to detail in older pieces. Look for things with fun collars, built-in belts, pockets, buttons, and pretty patterns.

3   **Consider versatility (in relation to price).** Be honest with yourself about how easily you can incorporate the dress into your existing wardrobe. Is it a simple pattern or color that you can wear with a bunch of things, or is it a bit more avant-garde? Based on how frequently you see yourself wearing it, be prepared to spend more or less accordingly.

wardrobe building blocks

Graduating from college had its challenges, like finishing my thesis, adjusting to a life without dining halls, and leaving behind a schedule that allowed me to work by the pool. And while the transition from school to a nine-to-five job wasn't easy, the thing that was hardest was developing a professional wardrobe.

Gone were the days of throwing on jeans, flip-flops, and an oversized sweatshirt before walking to class. Instead, I was expected to show up on a daily basis looking put together and professional; that's hard to do when the majority of your clothes are casual.

One of the most frequently asked questions that I receive is how to build a well-rounded wardrobe. Though most often this comes from recent college grads, it's something that everyone struggles with, and it can be a really intimidating process. So whether you're right out of school, a young professional, or a new mom, some general rules apply.

I first like to break things down into two main categories: Casual and Polished.

casual

Casual dressing is a bit of a balancing act. You want to look relaxed and comfortable, but without resorting to sweat suits and flip-flops. I find that most women have plenty of casual things in their closets—broken in jeans, plain T-shirts, and other loungewear that's mainly appropriate for home or the gym. The key is to have versatile pieces that can take you from an early-morning coffee run to a shopping date with girlfriends to a low-key dinner. See the chart on the opposite page for a sample inventory of a well-rounded casual wardrobe to help you determine your own essential pieces.

polished

Most people have more than enough casual pieces in their closet (I'm one of them). But when it comes to more polished or professional items, it's a lot more complicated. It isn't enough just to own a suit and a strand of pearls. See the chart for the items you need on hand to add a polished edge to any ensemble.

	polished	casual		polished	casual
tops	• White button down	• Striped T-shirt	**outerwear**	• 2 blazers	• Army jacket
	• 2 colorful blouses	• Chambray shirt		• Trench coat	• Wrap sweater
	• Pattern blouse	• 2 V-necks		• Leather jacket	• Vest
	• Silk blouse	• 2 scoop necks		• Faux fur jacket	• Grandpa sweater
	• Billowy blouse	• Neutral boatneck		• Peacoat	• Poncho
	• Embellished tank	• Relaxed tank top		• Tweed jacket	• Capelet
	• Sequined shirt	• Skin-tone camisole		• Cashmere sweater	• Puffy jacket
	• Lace top	• 2 long sleeve t-shirts		• Wool fedora	• Beanie
dresses	• Shirtdress	• White sundress	**accessories**	• Collar necklace	• Oversized watch
	• Leather detailing	• Printed cotton dress		• Costume earrings	• Bangles
	• Wrap jersey dress	• Strapless dress		• Bright cocktail ring	• Simple studs
	• Silk dress	• Maxi dress		• Diamond/cz studs	• Thin gold ring
	• 2 cocktail dresses	• Tank dress		• Metal aviators	• Scarf
	• 2 LBDs	• Sweater dress		• Thin patent belt	• Plastic rim sunglasses
	• Lace dress	• Bright tunic		• Leather bracelet	• Worn in belt
	• Embellished dress	• Striped dress			
shorts/ skirts	• Leather shorts	• Denim cut-offs	**shoes**	• Round toe pump	• Ballet flats
	• Crisp, tailored shorts	• Bright chino shorts		• Pointy toe pump	• 2 pairs flat sandals
	• Leather skirt	• Maxi skirt		• High heeled tall boot	• Short, flat boots
	• Pencil skirt	• Cotton skirt		• High heeled bootie	• Sneakers
	• Peplum skirt	• Pleated mini skirt		• Evening sandal	• Wooden wedge
	• Sequined skirt	• Printed flouncy skirt		• Platform sandal	• Tall, flat boot
bags	• Structured tote	• Relaxed satchel	**pants**	• High-waisted jeans	• Boyfriend jeans
	• Ladylike bag	• Cross-body bag		• Dark skinny jeans	• Relaxed skinny jeans
	• Small evening clutch	• Oversized clutch		• Wool trousers	• Colorful chinos
	• Leather carryall	• Straw/canvas tote		• Tapered trousers	• Leggings
				• Classic black pants	• Casual silk pants

when to splurge or save

Since most of us don't have unlimited funds for shopping, it's important to decide which things are worth saving up for and those that can be purchased for less. The items that you spend or save on should depend largely on your lifestyle, but these are my priorities:

spend: Shoes, bags, sweaters, coats, lingerie, trench coat, scarves, jeans.

save: Sunglasses, jewelry, hats, belts, blouses, tights, trendy items.

shifting wardrobe: summer to fall

One of the most challenging things about the transition from summer to fall clothing is that you have to do it in the middle of summer. That's when the new fall merchandise hits shelves, so even if you're currently wearing breezy tunics and sandals, it's important to think ahead, or all of the great pieces will be gone.

do your research
Either read magazines or look on blogs. It helps to be as organized as possible, so that you're aware of what's in your closet and you don't end up buying any repeats. For example: think of colors, shapes, textures, patterns, and overall feel ('70s minimalist, structured and neutral, or flowy and bohemian). A sample list: high-waisted trousers, slouchy knits (in either white or cream), oversized clutch, and leopard-print booties.

buy now, wear later
Just because you buy new items doesn't mean you have to wear them immediately (and if the weather is hot, you won't be that tempted). Instead, fold them up and put them in some sort of bin until they're seasonally appropriate.

edit your closet
Each new season makes for the perfect opportunity to edit your current wardrobe to make room for new pieces. Look through your items from the year prior and get rid of any that show signs of age. If you find a piece that's no longer current or on trend, donate that as well (unless, of course, it's vintage and/or expensive, in which case you should store it somewhere safe).

incorporate gradually
The transition from summer to fall is usually a gradual one; you probably won't need to be wearing an eyelet dress one day and a turtleneck the next. I like to incorporate fall pieces with my summer wardrobe in subtle ways, so that if I'm wearing a silk dress on a chilly night, I'll throw on a pair of tights with platform sandals. This way, you can extend the wear of some of your summer pieces without immediately transitioning to your fall wardrobe. Here I have added a blazer, tights, and booties to one of my favorite summer outfits, making it entirely suitable for cooler weather.

beauty

Summer beauty should be easy. Put away your blow-dryer and set aside your full-coverage foundation—your routine should embrace (faux!) bronzed skin, tousled hair, and brightly colored toes.

5 summer beauty must-haves for any budget

1

Hair: texturizing spray (used on wet hair for relaxed, beachy waves). Splurge: Bumble and bumble's "Surf Spray." Steal: Garnier's "Wonder Waves."

2

Face: cheek stain (adds a nice burst of color to glowy skin). Splurge: Tarte's "Dollface." Steal: Almay's "Smart Shade Blush."

3

Body: self tanner (to keep you out of the sun but still give you bronzed, even skin). Splurge: TanTowel. Steal: Neutrogena's "Build a Tan."

4

Lips: light pink gloss (illuminates your face in the most natural way). Splurge: Buxom's "White Russian." Steal: Neutrogena's "Whisper."

5

Nails: bright shades of coral/ orange (for your fingers and toes). Splurge: Deborah Lippmann's "Girls Just Want to Have Fun." Steal: OPI's "Don't Be Koi with Me."

* All Splurge items are shown on the left, Steal items on the right.

how to: manicure

Getting a professional manicure and pedicure is one of life's simple pleasures— and it's only made better with the addition of girlfriends and trashy magazines. It's indulgent, fun, and, best of all, you leave the salon feeling put together and polished (no pun intended). The one downside? Even the most affordable salons start to add up over time. Here's what you need to know in order to give yourself a professional-quality manicure at home.

Just as you prepare a room for painting (by sanding, filling gaps, and priming), you should do the same with your nails. If you simply slather on polish without doing anything else, it's going to look like you did it with your eyes closed. Although the preparation is time consuming, it's worth the effort.

tools

Cotton pads
Nail polish remover
Heavy hand cream
Manicure stick
Cuticle trimmer
Nail clipper
Nail file
Buffer
Nail polish
Top coat

1 Soak a cotton pad in polish remover and remove all old polish, making sure that it's completely gone (don't forget the areas around and underneath the nail). Wash your hands with soap and water.

2 Apply a heavy hand cream to your cuticles, and then gently push your cuticles back with a manicure stick.

3 Using your cuticle trimmer, clip the parts of your cuticle that are dry and ragged.

4 Clip your nails, and then file them to the desired length.

5 Run the buffer back and forth over the surface of your nail to smooth out any lines (this creates an even surface so that the polish adheres better).

6 Apply the nail polish using as few strokes as possible (I usually try to do one down the middle and one on either side), so that the nail is coated evenly, but not so that it's too thick. Apply a second coat using the same motions.

7 Apply one layer of the top coat, and let it dry.

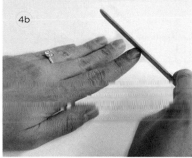

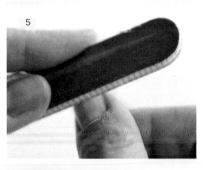

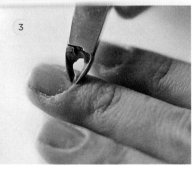

nail color

Women used to coordinate the color of their bags with their shoes (and sometimes the entire outfit), and the same used to be the case with fingernails and toenails. While there's nothing wrong with wearing the same color nail polish on both your fingers and toes, I prefer instead to wear different colors that complement each other. Here are some of my favorite combinations:

- peach and gray
- black and ballet pink
- lime green and bronze
- red and tangerine
- pastel lavender and robin's egg blue
- white and gold
- nude and dark red
- pink and metallic silver

how to:
tousled waves

I never put too much effort into my beauty routine in the summer. Between the heat and humidity, it's kind of a lost cause, and nobody wants to spend an extended amount of time in front of the mirror. Instead, I rely on easy makeup (sunscreen, tinted moisturizer, and mascara) and tousled, beachy waves.

My curling iron tutorial is my blog's most popular post of all time. After receiving countless thank you e-mails, I've come to realize just how many women are perplexed or intimidated by curling irons. Not only are they slightly dangerous (I've singed my ears and face more times than I'd wish to recall), but also, if used incorrectly, they can yield quite unattractive results—like harsh Shirley Temple-esque curls or crispy prom-night tendrils. Following my simple steps will give you natural, unfussy waves.

If you're in the market for a curling iron, I would recommend buying one of the new versions that come without a clamp (it's unnecessary and only gets in the way). Also consider the length of your hair and your desired wave size, then pick a curling iron size that works for you. The general rule of thumb is this: short hair = 1-inch barrel, medium hair = 1.5-inch barrel, and long hair

= 2-inch barrel. I'm a big fan of Hot Tools' 1.5-inch version—it's a good generic curling iron and suits my needs (even though it does have the clamp, which I removed). If you're new at using a curling iron, try practicing with it when it's not plugged in. It's a lot less scary and can help you get comfortable handling the tool.

There are two main looks that you can end up with when using a curling iron for tousled waves. The curls can be sleek and smooth or slightly messy and voluminous. The main difference is the state of your hair when you begin. If you've blown it out and used a flat iron so that it's super straight, you'll get less volume, but sleeker strands. If you curl hair that's been air-dried, you'll get more texture and body.

tools

Curling iron
Shine serum
Hair spray

1. Part your hair down the middle. Separate the very front section into a bun and secure with a rubber band.

2. Starting in the front, take a 2-inch section of hair and wrap it around the barrel of the iron (don't use the clamp). Curl the hair away from your face. Hold it in place for 10 to 20 seconds (or until the wrapped hair feels hot to the touch).

3. Slide the curling iron down and tug on the bottom of the hair just slightly to loosen up the curl so that it's more of a wave.

4. Continue around your head, repeating the same steps for every 2-inch section of hair.

5. When the bottom portion is curled, unwind the bun and begin curling the top portion.

6. Once all your hair has been curled, rake your fingers through it from root to tip. This will break up the curls and make them look more natural. Add shine serum (I like Frizz-Ease or Moroccan Oil) and work it throughout your hair. If you have any flyaways, spritz a little hair spray into the palm of your hand and gently run it over the strands until your hair is perfectly smooth.

at home

In the summer, I'm all about having a clean place with little clutter. Since we often host casual get-togethers in the summer, it's an ideal time to decorate, so our place always feels party-ready. Whether you're looking to fill your home with art or to organize a bookshelf, it's a great way to take advantage of long days.

defining your interior design style

My main motto for decorating is simple: incorporate things that you love, make it comfortable, and keep it clutter-free. If you're moving into your first apartment or simply wanting to spruce up your current space, implementing some little changes will make a big impact.

Determine your style. Do you gravitate toward modern pieces with a glamorous touch, or are you a fan of vintage chic? Once you have a better idea of your style, it will help identify the pieces you own that don't exactly fit and to determine whether a potential buy is a smart purchase.

Work with what you've got. If you have an old wooden desk that you can't stand, ask yourself if a new coat of paint (maybe something unexpected like a glossy orange) will make it appealing. If you have an ugly lamp, will a new lamp shade (or just adding a grosgrain ribbon along the base) make all the difference? Think of ways you can improve upon what you already own to save money and to create something customized to fit your needs.

Display your favorite items. Construct unique spaces that feel personal and aesthetically pleasing. For example, keep trays around to corral your favorite knickknacks, whether they include jewelry, perfume, candles, or artwork. Instead of keeping all your books on a bookshelf, stack them up on an unused chair and rest a figurine on top. It's all about finding ways to showcase your favorite things in slightly unpredictable ways.

Use fragrance. Candles are an obsession of mine, as they not only smell amazing, but they also create a beautiful ambience. (For dinner parties, though, I stick to unscented versions and light a scented candle only in the bathroom.) In the same way that people associate you with a certain perfume or scent, you should do the same for your home. My favorite candles are Diptyque's "Baies" and "Tubereuse," Manuel Canovas's "Palais d'Été," and Capri Blue's "Aloha."

Lighting is everything. To start, make sure any overhead lighting has great lightbulbs (the nonfluorescent variety). Light that is dull or too bright not only creates a harsh atmosphere, but also makes people's skin look sallow. In addition to overhead lights, place lamps at different heights around the room (it creates good dimension in addition to a well-lit space).

FILTH
IRVINE WELSH
Author of Trainspotting

ISLAM BOOK

PRIVATE PARTS

COLLECTED POEMS

THE THEORY OF POKER David Sklansky
I WILL TEACH YOU TO BE RICH
Mothering
THE BOY WHO
HARNESSED THE WIND
god is not Great Christopher
How Religion Poisons Everything Hitchens
Advertising   Planning
The MenisHealth Guide to
Peak Conditioning

breaking
dawn
STEPHENIE
MEYER

ARTIE LANGE

ULTIMATE DUMBBELL GUIDE

HOW IT ENDED

Daniel Silva
The Messenger

ATLAS
SHRUGGED
AYN RAND

KILLSHOT

SUPER SYSTEM
A COURSE IN POWER POKER
Doyle Brunson

MICHAEL CRICHTON
THE LOST WORLD

Al Franken
LIES
And the
Lying Liars
Who Tell
Them

At Memory's Edge

JAMES DEAN

LEE CHILD
THE HARD WAY

Jennifer Weiner
the grey zone

Running with Scissors

PHOTOGRAPHY

7 HABITS
HIGHLY EFFECTIVE PEOPLE

THE HOT ZONE RICHARD PRESTON

Web Metrics

MONEYBALL MICHAEL LEWIS

FANTASTIC VOYAGE
TERRY GROSSMAN

501 SPANISH VERBS

NTC's Beginner's
Spanish and English Dictionary

THE RULE of FOUR

JUSTICE GENDER FAMILY

EAT, PRAY, LOVE

NINE STORIES

Search Engine Optimization

Choke Chuck Palahniuk

GEOFFREY
GIULIANO   The BEATLES ALBUM
JAMES DEAN

shelve it— organizing a bookshelf

I've always had bookshelves in the places I've lived (from my room at my parents' house to my dorm in college), but I used to use them mainly for storing books, instead of as part of the overall decor. Not only do the things that you put on display tell a lot about who you are, but how you display them is equally important. Think beyond just lining books up side-by-side, categorized by subject. Here are some of my tips (expanded from one of my blog's most popular posts) for creating an organized bookshelf that is as functional as it is aesthetically pleasing.

Take note of what you already own. That way, you'll have a better idea of how to put it all together. Do you own mostly hardcovers, large books, thin books, entire series, or travel guides? Think of the books that make sense to group together (like cookbooks) and those that can be separated out and more creatively displayed.

Focus on interesting details (like the colors of the books) and group things together based on similar hues. This creates interesting depth and different focal points in a bookshelf.

Separate books that have truly unique covers and use them as displays. Instead of hiding the covers, turn the books so that they face outward. This adds character to your shelves and is a great way to display the books that might have special meaning. For example, I display the cover of my copy of *The Catcher in the Rye*. It's beat-up and the pages are falling out, but that's what makes it really pop.

Get creative. When arranging books, don't just line them up and fill up the entire shelf. Turn some books over on their sides, use bookends, and lean some diagonally. It's much more interesting to look at a bookshelf that has some variation.

Think beyond books. Do you have a piece of art that doesn't have a place or perhaps a beautiful vase that you never remember to use? Those are great pieces to add to a bookshelf to keep it from looking too much like a library. Disperse them around evenly, using them in lieu of bookends or setting them atop stacks of books. Collections work especially well; this is a great way to display them.

Combine old and new. One of my favorite aspects of being in a library is how many old treasures you uncover among newly published works. I try to implement that same concept with my bookshelves and the nonbook items I put on them—I might, for example, juxtapose a glossy vase with a rickety ladder.

7 **Nothing is off-limits.** In fact, the more outlandish items are on your bookshelf, the better! This also applies to things that would normally be kept in closets or under beds. Instead of keeping my childhood books and board games hidden, I display them. They add a fun contrast and a lived-in feel—like you could break out a board game on a whim.

8 **Customize.** Don't be afraid to add personalized elements to your bookshelf. Whether you paint the backing of the shelf a bright color, add a pattern to the trim, or install sconces, little touches make a big difference. You can even customize your books, by wrapping hardcover volumes in paper. I like the idea of keeping them all relatively coordinated, so I'd stick to one color scheme (like plain butcher paper, white wrapping paper, or something that has a great pattern).

food and entertainment

Summertime food has an almost unfair advantage over other seasons. Everything tastes better when it's eaten outside—whether at the beach, on a picnic blanket, or simply at a backyard barbecue. I've included some of my favorite recipes and techniques for things like the perfect piecrust and a refreshing orange-lime margarita.

summer
nostalgia party

When I was a kid, summer vacation was a magical time. Each day was filled with new adventures—my hair was perpetually green from the pool, and my hands were a sticky mess from ice cream. The same, unfortunately, can't be said of summertime as an adult. That's why I like to have a party celebrating all the nostalgic childhood memories I love most—I center the event around board games and treats I enjoyed as a kid. If you have access to an outdoor space, whether it's a beach, local park, or just your backyard, it will help get you in the frame of mind of a true summer vacation.

what to bring

drinks

Serve up the same drinks you enjoyed as a kid—but kicked up a notch. Whip up batches of Kool-Aid (with tequila), Yoo-hoo (with rum), or High-C (with vodka). It's a great way to create a fun atmosphere that will bring people childlike excitement. Also be sure to stock up on old-school sodas in glass bottles, and if you have access to a freezer, root beer floats are always a big hit.

food

Keep things simple and plentiful, with hamburgers and hot dogs and other old-school treats. Favorites include Fruit Roll-Ups, Goldfish, Circus Animal Cookies, Doritos, and of course, S'mores.

decor and activities

Bring plenty of places to sit—I like the idea of bright beach towels or picnic blankets. As for entertainment, a piñata or a game of Twister will help set the mood, as will a stereo playing old summer hits.

summer socializing

Summer also lends itself so well to informal get-togethers, since long, hot days guarantee a certain level of casualness. One of my favorite ways to host guests is to invite them for late-afternoon cocktails and appetizers. There's a lot less pressure when dinner's not involved, and almost all of it can be prepared in advance.

sugar cookies

I usually don't bother with cookies unless they're made with chocolate. The one exception is sugar cookies, and that's entirely thanks to royal icing. Most people tend to decorate cookies for the holidays, but they're an even more unexpected surprise during other times of the year. I love the idea of an icing that's customizable; you can use a variety of colors, add fun accoutrements, and turn them into little works of art (like these watermelon cookies that evoke the flavors of summer).

Baking homemade sugar cookies and decorating them is a process, but one that's completely worth it. The results are beautiful; they keep well in a covered container and always make great gifts. If possible, divide up the process into several stages, since making the dough, baking the cookies, and decorating them in one day can be quite an ordeal. After I make the dough, I wrap it in wax paper, and then just throw it in the fridge until I have time to roll out the cookies and bake them.

ingredients

Makes roughly 3 dozen cookies

- 3 cups all-purpose flour
- 1 teaspoon baking powder
- ¼ teaspoon kosher salt
- 1 cup unsalted butter, softened
- 1 ½ cup sugar
- 1 egg, beaten
- 1 tablespoon milk
- 1 teaspoon vanilla extract

1. In a large bowl, sift together flour, baking powder, and salt. Set aside.

2. In the bowl of an electric mixer, add butter and sugar and beat until smooth.

3. Add egg, milk, and vanilla to butter-sugar mixture and beat to combine. With the mixer on low speed, slowly add flour, and beat until mixture pulls away from the side of the bowl.

4. Divide the dough in half, wrap in wax paper, and refrigerate for 2 hours (the dough needs to be very cold in order not to stick to the cookie cutters or working surface).

5. Preheat oven to 375°F. Sprinkle working surface and rolling pin with flour. Remove the wrapped dough from refrigerator and roll out to ¼-inch thick.

6. Cut into shapes and place 1 inch apart on a parchment-paper lined baking sheet.

7. Bake for 8 to 10 minutes or until cookies just start to turn golden around the edges.

8. Remove from oven and let sit on baking sheet for 5 minutes and move to cool completely on a wire rack. Once cool, ice cookies (see following page).

royal icing

1 In the bowl of an electric mixer, combine the icing ingredients. Beat them together for 8 minutes on a low speed. The consistency of the icing should be similar to toothpaste (soft, but stiff enough to hold its shape).

2 If you're going to have several frosting colors, put them into separate bowls and add food coloring. Put the colored frosting into the squeeze bottles.

3 Using a squeeze bottle filled with icing, trace around the edge of each cookie (make sure you don't go all the way to the sides). Then "flood" (or fill) the inside of the cookie with icing, using either the tip of the applicator or a toothpick to help spread it so the surface is smooth and even.

4 At this point, you can leave the cookie as it is or add fun details, like a scattering of sprinkles or colored sugar. You can also let the first layer of icing dry completely, then layer other colors on top.

5 Serve the cookies or package them in clear cellophane bags tied with a cute ribbon to give as gifts.

tools

Bowls (to mix different icing colors)
Food coloring
Squeeze bottles with a
wide opening and a thin tip
   (to make the icing process infinitely easier)
Toothpick (to make fun designs and to help
   blend icing)
Topping accessories such as sprinkles,
edible pearls, and sugar candies (optional)
Colored sugar (optional)

recommended time line for easy cookie decoration

• **One or two days in advance:** If you can, make the dough.
• **The day before:** Roll the dough and cut out shapes with cookie cutters. Bake and cool the cookies and store them in an airtight container .
• **The day of serving:** Make icing and frost the cookies.

ingredients

Makes enough icing for roughly 3 dozen cookies

• 4 cups sifted powdered sugar
• 3 tablespoons meringue powder
• About 10 tablespoons warm water

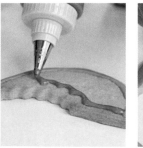
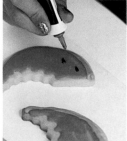

very berry pie with the perfect piecrust

I come from a pie-eating family. Don't get me wrong; I love a good piece of cake, but there's nothing that feels quite as celebratory as a freshly baked pie (served with ice cream, of course). My mom is an incredible baker, which makes me picky when it comes to the pies that I eat. I barely knew there was such a thing as store-bought piecrust until I attempted to make my own pie in college (it was a disaster). Since then, my mom has relayed some of her tips for getting a light and flaky crust (which is so good it consistently outshines the pie's filling). If you use fresh ingredients, though (like these berries I picked up at the peak of summer), there's nothing better.

ingredients

Makes 1 pie

crust

- 2 cups sifted all-purpose flour, plus more for rolling the dough
- ¾ teaspoon salt
- ¾ cup cold all-vegetable shortening (I always keep Crisco sticks in the freezer)
- 2 tablespoons chilled unsalted butter
- 8 to 10 tablespoons ice water

filling

- 5 cups mixed berries (I use raspberries, blackberries, and blueberries)
- 1 tablespoon lemon juice
- ¾ cup sugar
- 4 tablespoons cornstarch
- 1 teaspoon grated lemon zest
- A pinch of salt

1 Sift and measure the flour and put it into a large bowl. Add salt and then whisk together. Cut the shortening and butter into small pieces and add them to bowl. Working with either a pastry blender or two knives, use a chopping motion to combine the butter and flour until they are mixed together and the texture resembles coarse cornmeal. Slowly sprinkle the water around the bowl while tossing with a fork. Add only enough water so that when pressed together, the dough holds its shape—it shouldn't feel wet. Without handling the dough too much, make two equal-sized balls. Shape them into flattened disks, wrap them in plastic, and refrigerate them for 30 minutes.

2 Wash and drain the berries, place them in a large bowl, and add the lemon juice on top. In a smaller bowl, combine the sugar, cornstarch, lemon zest, and salt and pour it over the fruit. Carefully mix the filling ingredients together (making sure not to break up the berries too much), and then let them sit for 15 minutes so the flavors incorporate. Preheat the oven to 400°F.

3 On a lightly floured surface, roll out one disk of dough until it's roughly 13 inches in diameter.

4 Place the pie plate upside down on top of the crust and flip the entire thing over. Carefully peel off the wax paper (if the crust begins to stick, put it in the fridge for a few minutes), then gently fit the dough into the plate.

5 Repeat the rolling process to shape the other dough disk into a 13-inch circle and cut it into ¾-inch strips.

6 Pour the filling into the pie shell.

7 Lay several parallel strips of dough on top of the filling, leaving about ½ inch of space between each one (it usually takes about 5 to 7 in order to span the width of the pie). Fold back every other strip halfway and place one long strip of dough perpendicular to the parallel strips across the middle of the pie. Unfold the folded strips over the perpendicular strip. Now take the strips that are going under the perpendicular strip and fold them back. Lay another perpendicular strip next to the first, leaving some space between the two. Unfold the folded strips again. Repeat this process, weaving in strips, until you have made a complete lattice pattern over the top of the pie.

8 Trim the extra dough from the sides and use a fork to crimp the edges. Bake the pie for about 45 minutes, or until the crust is dark or the fruit bubbles over the top.

tips and tricks for pie making

- With piecrust, it's important to have everything as cool as possible (the colder the ingredients, the flakier the crust).
- Resist the urge to play with or mold the dough. The less you touch it, the better it will turn out.
- If the outer crust starts to brown too quickly in the oven, fold little pieces of aluminum foil around the edge to slow down the cooking process.

- Don't be afraid to mix different kinds of seasonal fillings.
- All fruit pie is best served warm and à la mode.
- If your pie doesn't come out looking perfect (or falls apart or gets too soupy or the like), don't stress. It will taste just as good scooped into a pretty bowl.

mint chip ice cream

When I was growing up, my parents made every season feel fun and full of little surprises. If it was cold outside, I'd come home to a cup of hot chocolate with marshmallows. On sweltering summer afternoons, we'd go out of our way to visit the local ice cream shop. I tend to lead my life in a similar way and find nothing more exciting during the summer than having a freezer full of icy treats (like refreshing granitas and old-school Popsicles).

I have a pretty standard ice cream maker (mine is by KitchenAid—basic models run around fifty dollars), and it was easily one of the best investments I've ever made. Some ice creams take a while to make, but others, like Mint Chip, take mere minutes. Here's my recipe for a seriously refreshing ice cream that combines the cool flavors of mint with a creamy base.

ingredients

Makes 2 quarts ice cream

- 2 cups milk (I use 2 percent)
- 2 cups heavy cream
- 1 cup granulated sugar
- ½ teaspoon salt
- 1 ½ teaspoons vanilla extract
- 1 tablespoon peppermint extract
- Green food coloring
- 1 cup chopped chocolate

1 Add the milk, cream, sugar, salt, and vanilla and peppermint extracts to a large bowl and stir until the mixture is completely blended. Slowly add in green food coloring until you get the desired color. I like it to be a very light mint green—nothing too drastic or neon—and this generally takes about 7 drops of coloring.

2 Follow the instructions that came with your ice cream maker to begin freezing the ice cream mixture. Once it has begun to freeze slightly, add in the chopped chocolate.

3 When the ice cream thickens to the right consistency, spoon it into a container and put it in the freezer until it is completely frozen, about 2 hours.

summer pasta with tomatoes, basil, and brie

For those nights when nothing sounds less appealing than spending time in a stuffy kitchen, this is my go-to dish. The sauce requires no cooking, and the flavor only intensifies the longer you let it sit. You simply stir tomatoes up with some herbs and cheese, let the mixture rest for a couple of hours, and toss it together with pasta.

ingredients

Serves 6

- 5 large tomatoes, cut into small cubes
- 12 to 16 ounces Brie, torn into small pieces
- 1 cup fresh basil, cut into strips, plus more for garnish
- 2 tablespoons fresh mint, cut into strips
- 3 garlic cloves, minced
- 1 cup olive oil
- 2 teaspoons salt
- Freshly ground pepper
- 1 pound angel hair pasta
- Freshly grated Parmesan cheese

1. In a large serving bowl, combine the tomatoes, Brie, basil, mint, garlic, olive oil, salt, and ½ teaspoon pepper. Let the mixture sit, covered, for an hour or two.

2. Meanwhile, bring a large pot of water to boil and cook the pasta until it's tender but still firm, following the directions on the package.

3. Drain the pasta and add it to the bowl of tomatoes; toss until well combined. Top with a sprinkling of fresh basil, Parmesan cheese, and pepper, and serve.

entertaining in summer

Summer is a great time to entertain. If the weather's nice, I always opt for gathering alfresco and keep extra blankets on hand in case it gets cooler later. I like the table to look really simple and go with all white linens with a few rustic touches (like raffia to tie the napkins). For appetizers, I prefer small, easy to eat snacks such as crostini, marcona almonds, olives, cornichons, and no-bake crudités.

stock up

I make a point of having a well-stocked bar that can accommodate people of all ages (and preferences). Here are some of my favorite things that I like to be able to offer my guests:

mixed drinks

Think of light, robust refreshments. Margaritas, sangria, fruit-based sodas, and champagne cocktails are always popular.

basic booze

Vodka, gin, and tequila (I think three options are sufficient). This obviously also depends on your tastes, so if you prefer rum or scotch, you can easily substitute those.

to keep chilled

Olives, beer, soda, and champagne (you never know when you'll need to celebrate!). Also, plenty of ice.

to keep on the kitchen counter

Lemons, limes, simple syrup (or just sugar), and maraschino cherries (perfect for dressing up a Shirley Temple or adding to a fancier drink).

glasses

Fancy glasses aren't necessary, and sometimes I find it more appealing when people use tumblers or mason jars for serving wine or iced tea, since it adds such a casual, rustic feel. The most important thing is to have enough glasses to accommodate different drinks. Don't worry if they don't all match!

little details

I like to offer flavored water (like mint, cucumber, and citrus) as an alternative to plain tap water. Once the water is filtered, I transfer it into glass bottles for a chic presentation.

summer cocktail: orange-lime margaritas

A summer cocktail should be bright and refreshing. My dad's orange-lime margaritas are always the perfect end to a hot, lazy day.

ingredients

Makes 1 cocktail

- Ice
- Freshly squeezed juice of 2 limes
- Freshly squeezed juice of ½ orange
- 2 ½ ounces tequila
- 1 ounce triple sec
- ¼ ounce agave syrup
- ¼ ounce Grand Marnier

In a cocktail shaker filled with ice, combine the lime and orange juices, tequila, triple sec, and agave syrup. Shake vigorously for 20 seconds. Strain the cocktail into a glass filled with fresh ice cubes and float the Grand Marnier on top.

Tipsy Tip: Keep a couple of cocktail glasses in the freezer at all times so you can serve icy cold drinks on a moment's notice.

03.
fall

Fall has always been my favorite season. It's full of anticipation and is a time to find joy in the subtle changes: switching to a heavy comforter, going apple picking, making homemade soup, and carving pumpkins with friends. It's also an ideal time for fashion, since mild weather supports a variety of choices, whether you opt for a lightweight dress balanced out by tights and boots, or an oversized sweater worn with bright lipstick for a look that's both comfortable and chic.

In this section you'll find recipes for crisp days, tips on how to wear one versatile piece multiple ways, ideas for entertaining (including a step-by-step guide to creating the ultimate Halloween soiree), beauty tutorials for unfussy but pulled-together looks, and ways to make your place feel cozy just in time to kick off the holidays.

style

After months of wearing breathable basics, I always welcome fall with open arms. It's a great time to pile on different pieces, creating layered looks that are complex and varied.

fall closet checklist

1   High-waisted trouser

2   Costume jewelry

3   Grandpa sweater

4   Leather skirt

5   Thicker rimmed sunglasses
    (opaque)

6   Military vest/jacket

7   Silk blouse (in a jewel tone)

8   Pencil skirt

9   Knee socks

10 Black wool short dress

11 Slouchy beanie

12 Long-sleeved shift

13 Animal-print skirt

14 Skinny black jeans

15 Oversized scarf

trendy behavior

I wouldn't categorize my style as being overly trendy. I'm aware of what's considered "in," but I don't wear things based solely on whether they've been deemed hip. Since I find a lot of people struggle with how to incorporate trends into their wardrobe, here's some guidance for how to wear current pieces without overdoing it.

• **Wear no more than two trends at once.** If animal prints, sequins, socks with sandals, faux fur, and bright lips are all the rage, pick one or two. Mixing them all together will look disheveled and desperate.

• **Incorporate different time periods and prices.** If you bought a great new pair of shoes, wear them with classic elements from your wardrobe. For instance, throw them on with a vintage dress and a belt you got a couple of seasons back to keep your ensemble from being one-dimensional. I also like to mix expensive + bargain items, so that my outfits never look too predictable.

• **Identify the trends that work for you.** During the summer of 2010, royal blue was all the rage. Sadly, it's just about the most unflattering shade that I can wear, so I passed on the trend altogether. If there's a shape or style that doesn't work for you, don't force it.

• **Know the time and place.** If you work in a conservative office, Monday morning is probably not the time to bust out your newest fluorescent shoes. Instead, save the of-the-moment trends for after hours, like when you're out at a restaurant with girlfriends or on a date.

pack a punch

Traveling and being away from home brings with it plenty of stresses, most of which begin with the process of packing. Whether you're unsure about what to bring, how to dress for the weather, or even essentials that you might not think to include, here are some tried-and-true tips.

- **Draw up a game plan.** If you're going on a road trip with friends or to a wedding that has a detailed itinerary, plan your outfits ahead. That way, you won't end up with four pairs of fancy heels in your bag when you only have to dress for one formal event. It really helps to make a packing list similar to the one on page 94.

- **Be prepared.** Check the weather report for your destination and consider contacting someone who lives in the area. Call a local boutique or hotel and ask them what the weather's like this time of year. As a native San Franciscan, I always advise people to bring "way more layers than they'd think necessary," when visiting the notoriously foggy city.

- **Pick a color palette and stick with it.** Focus on packing primarily neutral colors with a few bright accent pieces. Even though you'll have a guide with the outfits you planned, it makes it easy to switch things around if everything's in the same general hue.

- **Choose layers.** It's the best way to prepare for unexpected weather and changes in plans (a blazer can instantly make a casual sundress fancy enough for a night out). Make sure you bring some fun accessories like a hat, a pile of bracelets, and some statement earrings, since they also can quickly transform an outfit.

- **Pack efficiently.** Since you'll most likely have a limited amount of space, take advantage of things that can serve multiple purposes. An evening clutch might double as storage for jewelry, and the toes of your packed shoes can be stuffed with makeup, socks, or toiletries.

- **Roll with it.** Instead of folding your clothes like you would in your drawers at home, roll them into little sausages. This avoids creases, creates more room, and makes it easier to see what you've packed.

- **Downsize toiletries.** Whether you're flying or driving, you don't need to lug around your biggest bottle of shampoo and your bulk-size lotion. Instead, always have small, reusable bottles available, so that you can fill them up with your everyday items and throw them in your bag. Make sure you squeeze all the air out of the bottles and cover the tips with tape to minimize leaking, and store everything in a clear Ziploc bag, so that if there are any spills, you won't ruin the contents of your suitcase.

- **Wear your bulky items.** Instead of trying to cram your jeans, boots, and sweater (or any other large items) into your suitcase, wear them while traveling. This will save room and also keep you warm, since planes tend to get chilly right after takeoff.

- **Bag it.** Make sure to slip in a few extra plastic bags to store dirty clothes, wet bathing suits, or newfound souvenirs.

- **Flag it.** Add something to the outside of your suitcase to set it apart, so it's easy to spot at the baggage claim. You can purchase a ready-made luggage tag or do something as simple as tying a brightly colored ribbon to the handle.

sample packing list

Location: New York
Dates: 9/10–9/17
Weather: mid 60s during the day, with a slight chance of rain

essentials
Identification—passport and/or driver's license
Wallet, pared down to just the essentials—credit card, debit card, cash ($200)
Purse

extras/random
Band-Aids
Pain reliever
Hand sanitizer
Earplugs (You never know how noisy a place will be!)

technology
Phone + charger
Computer + charger
iPod and/or iPad + charger
Bose headphones + extra batteries
Camera + charger + battery pack

accessories
Lightweight scarf
Headband
Belts (2)
Sunglasses (2)
Jewelry (2 rings, 1 watch, 2 necklaces)
Tights (2)
Bags—carry-on (1), clutch (2)

shoes
Booties
Ballet flats
Heels (3)

clothes
Bras (3)
Underwear (12)
T-shirts (4)
Blouses (3)
Skirts (4)
Dresses (5)
Blazer
Sweaters (2)
Jeans
Trousers (2)
Sleepwear
Thick socks (good for the plane ride)

wearable wardrobe— one piece, multiple ways

The key to having a functional wardrobe is to invest in classic pieces that can be worn a variety of ways. Things like neutral-coloured blazers, black dresses, and white blouses are always good to have on hand, but my leather skirt is easily the most versatile piece I own. With just a few simple changes, it can transition from day to night, and it's surprisingly current, no matter what the season.

clothes for your lifestyle

To figure out which pieces in your closet will get the most use, have a realistic view of your lifestyle. It's all about calculating the cost per wear, so that even if you purchase an exorbitantly priced purse, if you carry it every day, it might make sense financially. If you often go out at night, invest in a great leather jacket that can also be worn over cotton basics during the day. The same can be said for someone who works in a conservative office and relies on classic, comfortable heels that are professional but playful enough so they can be worn out to a dinner date. Most important, before you make the investment, know which items will get a lot of use (a beautiful ball gown does you no good if it only collects dust in the back of your closet).

photograph pretty

Unless you're one of those people who manage to look incredible in every picture, you're probably uncomfortable in front of the camera. I used to be one of those girls who would shimmy to the back of the crowd, since far too often I'd be disappointed in how I looked. I'm not a model, but after having had my picture taken thousands of times for my blog, I've developed a few tricks that anyone can use to increase the chance that a photo will be flattering.

1 **Spend some time in front of the mirror.** This is one of those things that feels terribly vain, but it's important. Everyone has a certain angle that's most flattering (mine is with my face turned to my right); this is just about figuring that out. Prior to learning my best angle, I'd usually stare straight on into the camera looking fish-eyed and awkward.

2 **Relax.** Most people instinctively tense up when having their pictures taken, so try to think of something that will help you stay calm. There's nothing cute about a forced smile, crazy eyes, and shoulders that are up to your ears. Take a deep breath, put your shoulders back, and relax.

3 **Think of something that makes you happy.** Corny? Most definitely. But more often than not, when I think of something joyful (like my cats, a recent vacation, or even the dessert I'm about to consume), I smile much more naturally. Act like you're smiling at someone you love and not simply posing for a photograph.

4 **Understand positioning.** If you pose facing straight toward the camera, your widest parts will be photographed. Instead, tilt your body just slightly, but turn your shoulders and face toward the camera. If you don't know how to make your body look natural (and also flattering), take a cue from actresses who get their pictures taken on the red carpet: They look confident, happy, and poised. Keep your arms in either a relaxed position by your sides or rest one hand on your hip. Keep your legs close together or put one foot in front of the other.

getting a leg up— tips on tights

Tights are among those seemingly simple accessories that are more complicated than most would think. In the past, I used to come home from the store with several options, only to find they were all too tight/sheer/uncomfortable/thick/thin. Once you understand how to find the right pair, though, tights are an easy way to keep warm while inserting a bit of style into a fall ensemble. Here are a few of my favorite ways to wear them.

- **Go dark.** I avoid sheer, transparent, and shimmery tights because they're not flattering on me, nor do they help keep me warm. Instead, I favor the opaque variety, as they're slimming and sleek. You can usually find out how solid they're going to be by checking their "denier" (the higher the number, the more opaque—I like 100 denier).

- **Create variety.** Though most of my tights are black, I like to have other options to add a pop of color to otherwise neutral outfits. Think of hues like charcoal gray, mustard yellow, cranberry, and forest green.

- **Go up a size.** It's not fun to go up a size in anything, but with tights, bigger is better. Small tights will stretch out and become more transparent, and you may end up with unflattering muffin tops at your waistline.

- **Add texture.** Instead of sticking only with smooth tights, choose some with texture, whether they're knitted, ribbed, or some sort of lacy pattern.

- **Incorporate summer footwear.** It may be chilly outside, but that doesn't mean you have to retire your favorite sunny-weather shoes until spring. Instead, add some juxtaposition to a cold-weather outfit by pairing tights with open-toed shoes. To keep it looking playful and funky, make sure the shoes have a sturdy, chunky heel.

beauty

To me, fall beauty is all about understated drama—bright lips, dark nails, and hair that's never too done so that it can't benefit from a perfectly placed hat.

5 fall beauty must-haves for any budget

1 **Hair:** hair spray (to help with all the static cling from knits/scarves/hats). *Splurge*: Sexyhair's "Smooth + Seal." *Steal*: L'Oréal's "Elnett Spray."

2 **Face:** metallic eye shadow (just a little bit—it goes a long way—to add a festive touch). *Splurge*: Buxom's "Pug." *Steal*: L'Oréal's "HIP Metallic Duo."

3 **Body:** exfoliating scrub (with an emollient to keep dry skin away). *Splurge*: La Licious's "Tahitian Flower Sugar Soufflé." *Steal*: St. Ives's "Apricot Scrub."

4 **Lips:** poppy, bright pink, or red (sunglasses and a swipe of vivid lipstick, for a casual chic vibe). *Splurge*: Nars's "Heat Wave." *Steal*: Maybelline's "Coral Crush."

5 **Nails:** vamp (because nothing looks more put together than dark nails and a statement watch). *Splurge*: Chanel's "Vamp." *Steal*: Essie's "Wicked."

* All Splurge items are shown on the left, Steal items on the right.

how to:
bright lipstick

Until recently, I was intimidated by the idea of wearing bright lipstick. I found it far too jarring and was convinced that it would be smeared across my teeth within minutes of putting it on. It's now one of my favorite makeup tricks, whether I'm going for a glamorous nighttime look or simply swiping on a punchy color before running errands.

bright lips: three ways

Since a lot of girls feel like they can't wear lipstick (definitely not the case!), here are three different ways you can embrace the look in a way that feels best to you.

a   **Lightly stained.** Put on chapstick and then use your finger and dab it onto a lipstick and add a single, thin coat to your lips. It should be subtly colored, almost as if you've just finished a Popsicle.

b   **One coat color.** Use a bright color (like apricot), and only apply one coat from the tube directly to the lips. This will still make an impact, but won't be blindingly bright.

c   **High impact.** Embrace a bold shade (like a vibrant orange or true red) and apply two coats from the tube directly to the lips. This should be the main focal point on your face, so make sure to keep the rest of the look subdued.

tools

Foundation
Light-reflecting lotion
Concealer
Bronzer
Eyelash curler
Glossy black mascara
Lip balm
Tissue
Bright lipstick

1 Create an even base using a combination of foundation and light-reflecting lotion (I find it's the best way to get the right amount of coverage that still looks natural).

2 Sweep on bronzer, concentrating on the forehead, down the nose, and along the cheekbones.

3 Curl your eyelashes and apply one coat of mascara (keep your eyes really minimal so you don't distract from your bright lips).

4 Apply lip balm and then blot with a tissue (this helps seal any cracks, but doesn't make lips too slick for the lipstick to adhere).

5 Apply the lipstick.

6 Place your index finger inside of your mouth and close your lips around it while sliding it back out (this will ensure your lipstick doesn't end up on your teeth).

how to:
fake eyelashes

Fake eyelashes are a great way to add major drama to your look. When done properly, they should make your eyes look incredible, but not costumey. The problem is, they're a bit tricky to master. I first put on a pair of fake eyelashes in high school for a homecoming dance, only to realize halfway through the night that they had begun to peel off (I didn't let the glue get tacky enough). I now follow these simple steps to ensure that they look great when I first apply them and don't budge until I wash my face before bed.

tools

Fake eyelashes
Small cosmetic scissors
Eyelash adhesive
Tweezers
Mascara
Black eyeliner (optional)

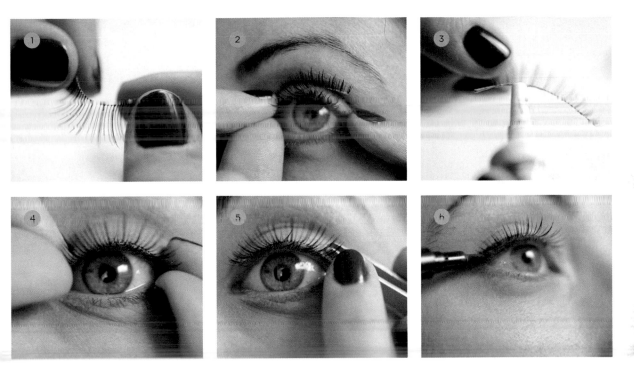

1 Remove the fake lashes (I like the versions by MAC and Ardell) from their container and bend them a bit to loosen them up. This bending will also help them maintain a shape closer to that of your eyelid.

2 Hold up the eyelashes to your eye to measure the length (the shortest lashes go toward the inner eye). If necessary, trim the lashes with the scissors so they're the same length as your eyelid.

3 Lightly apply a thin layer of adhesive (I use Duo's dark version) along the rim of the fake eyelashes (or put a dollop on a piece of tissue and use a Q-tip to apply), focusing on the outer edges, and then wait 30 seconds to ensure that the adhesive is tacky and will stick.

4 With your eyes just partially closed (this gives you the best angle), hold the fake eyelashes at either end (while maintaining the general shape of your eye) and line them up with your eye. Gently apply the fake lashes, trying to position them as close to your natural lashes as possible. Hold them still for 15 seconds, concentrating on the ends, so that they adhere.

5 With your tweezers, gently press down on the fake eyelashes (toward your own natural lashes), so they blend in.

6 Add a coat of mascara to both your natural lashes and the fake ones. Add a thin layer of black eyeliner along the top of your eye, which will make the lashes really pop.

at home

Fall is a great time to get inspired and polish up the feel of your interior space. Take care of a few of those things you've been putting off, like finding an attractive way to display one of your collections, so that when winter comes, you can cozy up in a home that is stylish and comfortable.

A complete overhaul isn't necessary in order to acknowledge the shift in seasons. Instead, a few simple changes will help transition your place from a sun-filled summer home into one that's inviting for fall. Easy fixes include draping a blanket over the sides of a chair, splurging on a nice heavier candle (avoid gingerbread, eggnog, sugar cookies, and peppermint as they're often saccharine), and switching out light and colorful pillows in favor of ones with more texture and darker hues.

inspired design— where to look

Since fall brings with it cool weather, I find I'm most inspired to switch things up in my place then, but before you make any drastic moves, you need a plan of attack. Much in the way that you should have a general idea of your aesthetic when it comes to dressing, the same applies to your home. It should have an overarching theme that plays throughout the year (whether this is midcentury modern meets glamour den or flea market chic meets downtown eclectic). Articulating your style will help you identify the things that truly fit within that scope—just in time for the holidays.

- **Compile images.** Create a file on your computer or a folder on your desk that's filled with images of things you like. Don't think about why you're drawn to them—it might be a bathroom floor's tiling or a glamorous living room. Great sources include magazines, books, old photographs, fabrics, artwork, and interesting fonts.

- **Sort through your images.** Look for themes and any recurring components, like all-white kitchens, rustic dining rooms, or serene bedrooms.

- **Take note of what you find and start labeling:** cozy, stark, clean, bohemian, simple, modern, vintage. From there, you should come up with a tagline of sorts that determines your aesthetic. For example, mine would be "streamlined and simple, with a vintage twist."

- **Keep lists.** I keep an ongoing list for things I'd like to change about my place that's categorized as "wants" and "needs." My current coffee table is far too big, clunky, and overpowering for the living room . . . but it's completely functional, and since I'm merely looking to upgrade, a new coffee table is a "want." However, in the guest room, I still don't have bedside tables, which I've categorized as a "need," since my visitors should have a light by the bed and a place to keep a glass of water. Having a running list of wants and needs helps you prioritize the things that are truly important over those that you'd like to upgrade, but that aren't absolutely critical.

- **Take pictures.** When there are components that are missing or things I'd like to change about a room, it's easier to see in photographs. For example, I took a picture of our bedroom. Looking at it helped me to identify the following:
  Like—bed placement, wall color, lamps
  Need—rug, headboard, art
  Change—nightstands

- **Analyze the problem spots.** Take note of things that don't work and decide whether they should be tossed (or donated) or whether they simply need some extra attention. I bought a beat-up bench from a flea market that had tattered fabric and ugly wood and transformed it with a few simple touches (see the following pages).

- **Don't forget the details.** Little things make a difference. For instance, good lighting is crucial. Change out any bulbs that have a harsh or unflattering glow, and think about whether light fixtures and lamps need to be updated or replaced. New rugs, flowers, plants, and freshly painted walls can dramatically improve a room's look.

riding the bench

Benches are great to have around the house for extra seating (ideal for larger than normal dinner parties) or to have in the bedroom for a place to put on shoes. I bought this bench (above, left) for $25 at a flea market and, with a few touches, transformed it into a sleek piece that looks chic and current (above, right).

tools

Tarp
Oil-based primer spray paint
Spray paint
Staple gun + staples
Fabric
Scissors

1 Remove the cushion and set aside. Prep the bench by wiping clean and sanding if necessary. Lay down a tarp and add a coat of oil-based primer and add two coats of paint (I prefer using spray paint, as I find it's quickest).

2 Lay the fabric on the floor (I found my Vera Wang fabric at a nearby fabric store).

3 Place the cushion face-side down. Trim the fabric so that it's roughly 5 inches wider than the cushion on all sides.

4 Center the pattern, if necessary, and pull the fabric taut over the edges (starting with the front and back) and staple it to the frame.

5 Secure the sides and make sure to overlap the corner pieces perfectly for streamlined edges.

6 Trim the extra fabric and place the cushion onto the bench frame.

collectibles

I used to think that displaying collections was old-fashioned and stale. And it definitely can be, if done incorrectly. When I was growing up, the mom of one of my friends collected mallard-themed objects, and every corner of the house was filled with duck statues, pictures, and stuffed animals. However, when chosen carefully and displayed in a calculated way, collections can showcase things you love while also infusing your own personality into a room.

Without even realizing it, most people collect items that can easily be grouped together in an intentional way. After returning home from the flea market two weeks in a row with antique globes in tow, it became apparent that I had started a collection, and they now live on the top of my bookshelves.

The best way to start a collection is to think about things you love that will make for an eclectic and interesting display—does your attraction revolve around music, art, food, fashion, or random knickknacks? I recently got into vintage brooches and pins and now keep them displayed all together in little dishes.

detailed decor

• **In every room:** Have one space that feels really pretty and polished, filled with things like candles and beautifully framed photographs, and accented by cute touches like a lingerie drawer with fragrant soaps or trays lined with your favorite objects (colorful nail polishes, special trinkets, and the like).

• **Your bedroom:** Make your bedroom space a tranquil environment. Collect things you love (I keep a stack of my favorite poetry books by my bed), put out fresh flowers, use a light fragrance (I like Alora's "Isola" room freshener). Set a bench at the end of your bed, if space permits; choose a pretty nightstand and place a little notepad by the bed (so you can write things down in the middle of the night). Most important, keep your bedroom clutter-free.

• **Guest bedroom:** Whether you have a guest bedroom or just a spare couch, make sure your guests feel comfortable with clean towels, flowers, new soap, books, water and a carafe, extra blankets, and toiletries.

food and entertaining

It's not an exaggeration when I say that I count the days until Halloween all year. That one day brings together so many of my favorite activities (costumes, carving pumpkins, eating candy, and watching scary movies) and helps kick off a season filled with wonderful holiday traditions. During this time, I find there's nothing more comforting than having something simmering on the stove that makes your entire place smell like home.

a haunting halloween

I take Halloween pretty seriously, which in itself is a bit of an oxymoron. But the truth is, it's a hard holiday to decorate for, since it very easily crosses the line into being cheesy. I went through that stage in college when every costume was a sexy fill-in-the-blank (devil, sailor, pirate, or French maid). I've since moved on from frat parties and revealing outfits to more elegant get-togethers that feel eerie but sophisticated.

themed entertaining

The two main things people expect at a Halloween party are good drinks and sweets, so be prepared with a few options. Here are some of my favorite ideas to incorporate them in a way that feels festive and fun.

drinks

Stick to one signature cocktail for the evening, and serve it in mason jars with a large chunk of dry ice on the bottom. It doesn't have to be complicated—think vodka soda with a splash of lime and then add a bit of food coloring to really set the scene. I line up drinks on chic mirrored trays that have been covered with moss and top them off with orange and black striped straws.

food

Halloween is an indulgent holiday, so don't skimp on the treats. I like to fill bowls with different candies (keep them separated out by kind—chocolate, fruity, etc.) and distribute them around the house for people to snack on throughout the night. I also like the look of themed cupcakes in different Halloween-appropriate colors (like black, orange, white, and green) stacked together on a tiered cake stand. Don't be afraid to incorporate creepy details within the desserts—like doughnuts crawling with (plastic) spiders or caramel apples infested with (gummy) worms.

decor

I stay away from anything that feels cutesy or obvious and instead focus on creating more of an eerie ambiance. The goal should be to have decorations that seem almost as though they could naturally be part of your decor. Great lighting is an easy way to start. I use black candles and candlesticks (I spray-painted a few mismatched candlesticks that I had), so that the look is cohesive. Trays that normally house pretty candles, books, and other trinkets can be loaded up with objects such as skulls or miniature pumpkins. Use fake insects to make it look like a lampshade is under attack, and dress up your bookshelves with a lone crow.

costume creation

Picking out a unique costume year after year is no easy feat. But with a few simple tricks (and knowing the right places to look for inspiration), you can be sure to have consistently creative get-ups each Halloween.

films
Head to your local movie store or go online and browse through films. Oftentimes, I'll remember a movie I was fond of when I was a kid (like *A League of Their Own*) or come across a cult classic (*The Breakfast Club* or *The Princess Bride*) that suggests a great costume. See above for my costume inspired by Hitchcock's *The Birds*.

tv
Turn to current TV listings (i.e., *Mad Men*) or classic shows (*I Love Lucy* or *The Mary Tyler Moore Show*) for inspiration. These are a great place to look for costumes—and it's even more fun to get a group together to do an ensemble cast.

books
If you're using literature for inspiration, pick a character from a classic book with an identifiable feature that a lot of people will recognize (like Holden Caulfield's red hunting cap in *The Catcher in the Rye*).

pop culture
Turn on the radio, pick up a magazine, or think of famous moments that would translate well into a costume.

perfect chocolate chip cookie

To me, a classic chocolate chip cookie is about as perfect as it gets. And while there are countless recipes out there, this one combines all of my favorite elements into one slightly crispy yet chewy cookie.

ingredients

Makes roughly 2 dozen cookies

- 2 ¾ cups all-purpose flour
- ½ teaspoon kosher salt
- 1 ¼ teaspoons baking soda
- 1 cup (2 sticks) unsalted butter, at room temperature
- 1 cup packed dark brown sugar (dark brown sugar has a lot more flavor than light)
- ½ cup granulated sugar
- 1 teaspoon vanilla extract (make sure it's not imitation)
- 1 large egg, at room temperature
- 12 ounces semisweet chocolate chips (at least 60 percent cacao content)

1 Whisk together the flour, salt, and baking soda in a bowl. Set aside.

2 In a large bowl, using an electric mixer or a stand mixer, beat the butter, sugars, and vanilla at medium-high speed until light and fluffy, about 3 minutes. Add the egg and mix until just combined.

3 With the mixer on low, gradually add the flour mixture in several batches and beat until incorporated. Stir in the chocolate chips, using a large spoon. Cover the bowl with plastic wrap and refrigerate the dough for 1 hour (this will help all the flavors really meld).

4 Preheat the oven to 375°F and line a baking sheet with parchment paper.

5 Drop mounds of cookie dough about 1 inch apart. I use a small ice cream scoop that's just slightly larger than 1 tablespoon to ensure that all the cookies are evenly sized. Bake the cookies for 13 to 15 minutes (rotating the sheet once halfway through), or until the edges are just slightly browned. Remove the sheet from the oven and let it stand for 5 minutes. Transfer the cookies to a wire rack to cool completely.

cookie crash course

These three simple tips will guarantee that your cookies come out just right every time.

1 Use the highest-quality ingredients you can—it makes a huge difference. That goes for eggs (I buy organic, from cage-free chickens whenever possible), vanilla extract (my favorites are Madagascar and Tahitian varieties), and chocolate (make sure it's at least 60 percent cacao content).

2 While most recipes call for the butter to be at room temperature, it's best if all the other ingredients are as well. Make sure to take your egg out of the fridge a little bit ahead of time so it can warm up.

3 Don't overmix. While you do want to make sure that the butter and sugars are beaten together very well, the other ingredients should be mixed just until they're combined— no longer. Overmixing the dough will result in flat, dense cookies.

homemade pizza dough

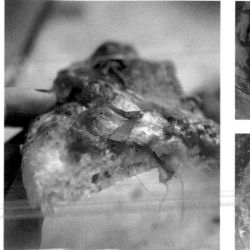

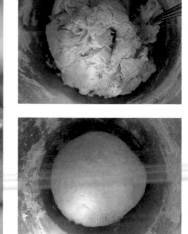

When I was growing up, one of my favorite dishes was my mom's homemade pizza. I found the entire process so comforting—helping her knead the dough, watching it rise in a yellow bowl that she'd put out in the front yard, and finally waiting for the finished pizza to come out of the oven. All you need are a few basic ingredients (most of which you should already have in your kitchen) and a little bit of time to let the dough rise.

ingredients

Makes enough for two 10-inch thin-crust pizzas

- ¾ cup warm water (it should be between 105°F and 110°F)
- 1 packet active dry yeast (not fast-acting)
- ½ teaspoon sugar
- 2 ½ cups all-purpose flour (you can also substitute part or all whole wheat)
- 2 tablespoons olive oil
- 2 teaspoons salt

1 Preheat the oven to its highest temperature (mine is 500°F).

2 Pour the warm water into a large bowl, sprinkle in the yeast and sugar, and let the mixture sit for 5 minutes until it's slightly bubbly. Stir in the flour, olive oil, and salt until it forms a ball (if it seems dry, you can add a teaspoon of water at a time until it comes together, but make sure it doesn't get overly sticky).

3 Place the dough onto a lightly floured surface and knead until it's smooth and elastic. Use the same bowl and drizzle in just enough olive oil to coat the bowl (so the dough doesn't stick). Place the ball of dough inside and cover it with a damp cloth. Let it rise for about 45 minutes, or until it's doubled in size.

4 If you're using a pizza peel (the long wooden paddle used to transfer pizza to and from the oven), sprinkle on a little cornmeal (this will help the pizza slide off onto the heated pizza stone in the oven) and roll the dough out to the desired size. Don't worry if you don't have these tools; simply sprinkle cornmeal onto a baking sheet and place the pizza directly in the oven.

5 Now you're ready to add your favorite toppings (I love the combination of sautéed onions, sage, and fennel sausage). When you've done that, bake the pizza until the bottom of the crust is golden brown and the cheese— if you've used any—is melted, roughly 7 to 10 minutes.

my favorite pizza

Once the dough has been rolled out, I add a thin layer of olive oil, and then two cloves of minced garlic. Spoon on canned tomato sauce (my favorite is Rao's) and add low-moisture shredded mozzarella cheese. Finish with a sprinkling of sea salt along the crust. Once the pizza is out of the oven, I add thin strips of fresh basil and finish with some red pepper flakes. It's great with a basic salad (I usually just dress some butter lettuce with my basic vinaigrette—see page 48) and open up a medium-bodied red wine.

tools

(helpful, but not necessary)

- Pizza peel (great way to transfer the pizza to the oven)
- Pizza stone (this gets really, really hot, so it helps make a crispy crust)
- Pizza cutter (easiest way to cut up a pizza)

autumnal decorating

I grew up in a house that had very few decorations around the holidays, mainly because my mom is strongly opposed to clutter. I tend to agree when it comes to my own place, but I love the idea of making my home feel seasonally inspired, without being corny or cartoonish. Halloween is my favorite holiday, but that doesn't mean I hang skeletons from every door. Instead, I stick to a few details that add an overall feel to the place, without being too literal.

Some of my favorite accent pieces include crows perched in high spots, skulls that can be used as centerpieces with dark flowers, hands that hold candles. Ultimately, think beyond the obvious (so instead of witches and goblins, think skulls and crows; instead of just orange and black, think black, gold, and dark purple).

For Thanksgiving, use natural elements as part of your table's decor. I place mini pinecones on each napkin with a little string attached to a tag (with each person's name) as a placeholder. It shows people to their seats in the most autumn-inspired way.

fall cocktail: classic vodka martini

It took years before I was able to appreciate the intricate, dry flavors of a well-made martini. Now I love making them for guests and much prefer their taste to that of sugary sweet cocktails. Best of all, martinis call for only two ingredients—and a garnish—and are among the easiest drinks to make.

ingredients

Makes 1 cocktail

- 2 ounces vodka
  (I like Ketel One)
- ½ ounce dry vermouth
  (I like Dolin)
- Lemon twist or olive

In a tall glass filled with ice, combine the vodka and vermouth. Using a long spoon, stir until the liquid is cold (about 25 rotations) and strain it into a chilled cocktail glass. Add a twist of lemon peel or an olive.

Tipsy Tip: For an indulgent topper, I like to stuff green olives with blue cheese and skewer them onto silver cocktail picks. It adds great flavor and brings a bit of color to the drink.

04.
winter

Winter brings with it such nostalgia—the electricity in the air around the holidays, family dinners, warm knits, the scent of pine trees and gingerbread, and the taste of candy canes and eggnog. It's such a wonderful time of year, but I've found that it can also be increasingly stressful the older I get. In an effort to avoid the mall on Christmas Eve and to actually enjoy the countless holiday parties that inevitably line up, I've learned that it's all about adequate preparation.

In this section, you'll find gift guides for all budgets, a lesson on how to write the perfect thank-you note, cozy items worth splurging on for your wardrobe and home, and how to host an Oscar party that everyone will want to attend.

style

With nonstop holiday parties and the promise of a glamorous New Year's Eve, it's important to have a closet that lends itself to lots of mixing and matching. I make sure to stock up on the layered basics that are perfect for warming up on dreary mornings.

In addition to shopping for warm sweaters and winter coats, it's also the season to assemble gifts for your friends and family. This chapter includes lots of advice on gift giving and stylish gift-wrapping ideas.

winter closet checklist

1. Faux-fur vest

2. Messenger bag

3. Tie-neck blouse

4. Heavy coat

5. Leather gloves

6. Sequined top/jacket/cardigan

7. Menswear-inspired blazer

8. Cape/poncho

9. Sweater dress

10. Winter white pants
    (in a heavier fabric)

11. Statement necklace

12. Textured skirt

13. Cashmere sweater

14. Beaded/sparkly clutch

15. Heeled booties (in black)

layering logistics

Growing up in California and having lived there my whole life, I wouldn't exactly call myself an expert when it comes to dressing for winter. But with that being said, I've spent a fair amount of time in colder climates, where I quickly learned some essentials for staying warm while looking chic.

invest in one great coat
Though you may be tempted to buy something trendy (like a crazy print or a specific cut), go with something neutral and classic that will last you several seasons (look to Burberry's classic trench for inspiration).

choose layers over bulk
Instead of relying on one thick jacket, wear lots of thin layers. This way, your look will be streamlined, chic, and, of course, less voluminous. See the photos opposite for one of my outfits that involves several layers. You can also stick to one color palette for your entire outfit for a monochromatic look once you shed your outer layers.

add accessories
Make them colorful, and choose an assortment of textures and prints. Add a textured knit hat with a patterned scarf and some leather gloves. The variety will add depth to your outfit, as well as making the entire look pop with fun accessories.

dressing the party

By the time December rolls around, my calendar is always jam-packed with events—a gingerbread house assembly get-together, office Christmas parties, and cocktail soirees. Each one requires a different ensemble, whether it's a sparkly dress for New Year's Eve or something casual to wear to a good friend's annual potato latke party. Regardless of the event, here are a few basic pieces I own that make it easy to dress up or down, depending on the occasion.

black cocktail dress
The key here is balance. It should be polished, but not too fancy; in a cut that's flattering, but not too showy; with enough details to make it feel special, but not so many that they overpower the dress. Look at this as your one investment piece that will be appropriate for a variety of events. Things to look for: silk chiffon/satin/cotton, hits just above the knee, tapered at the waist. Things to avoid: too tight, too short, too heavy (people usually crank up the heat during parties).

sparkly jewels
There's nothing that elevates a party outfit quite like a pair of statement earrings, a dazzling bib necklace, or a great cocktail ring. Once you decide on your main dress for the season, pick an accessory that really complements your piece. If the dress has a high neckline, throw on a necklace that will play up your face, or a stack of shimmering bangles to add a bit of dimension to your look.

festive heels
While comfort is obviously key when picking out a pair of heels, particularly if you live in a snowy/rainy locale, you also want to make sure you're looking your best. Pick a shoe that has a good platform in front (at least 1 inch) and don't be afraid of details like cut-outs or ankle straps, and fabrics like velvet. Also, have fun with tights. While black opaque stockings are always a great choice, don't be afraid to add a punchy color or textured/patterned tights (see page 101 for more on tights).

baggage
You don't need to lug around your normal day-to-day objects to a holiday party, so leave your big purse at home and take an evening bag. Here are my criteria for a perfect clutch: removable shoulder strap (sometimes it looks chicer to go without, other times it's convenient when you're balancing a drink and food), just large enough to fit the basics (cash, credit card, lipstick, keys, phone, and breath mints), and festive (either in a ruched satin or with sparkles—I can never get enough sequins).

cover-up
Since a dress and tights aren't exactly weather-appropriate in midwinter, it's important to invest in a great piece that you can throw on over your ensemble. Depending on just how cold it is, I like faux fur capelets, wool coats in unexpected colors (like poppy red or emerald green), a classic peacoat, or a couple of layers (like a cashmere sweater and a leather jacket).

Whether you keep these in your bathroom cabinet or the glove compartment in your car, these are my essentials for remedying fashion disasters, from missing buttons, to blisters, to sudden spills.

Lint brush
Tide To Go Instant Stain
 Remover
Bobby pins
Sewing kit
Safety pins
Q-Tips
Band-Aids
Cotton balls
Floss

navigating neutrals

In the same way that people wholeheartedly embrace bright colors in the warmer months, neutrals often become the go-to shades during the winter. There are ways to wear muted colors, though, without the whole look feeling stagnant or boring. Here are some of my favorite methods of incorporating neutrals into my winter wardrobe.

head to toe
Embracing one color or tone from head to toe (whether it be cream, black, or my favorite, heather gray) makes a statement. The colors don't have to match perfectly, but instead, try to find certain elements and fabrics that complement each other. Example: gray slouchy sweatshirt + grayish wool trousers + gray snakeskin clutch. Even though the same color is used throughout, the different textures keep it feeling fresh and fun.

winter white
Though white jeans should be reserved for beachside barbecues in the summer (unless, of course, you really toughen them up with a black motorcycle jacket, slouchy sweater, and ankle boots), it's now completely appropriate to wear this crisp color any time of year. Whether you invest in a snow-white coat, a mohair sweater, or a creamy wool skirt, it'll be a great way to brighten dreary days.

black with metallics
On chilly days, I'm almost always drawn to black basics. Black is easy, you don't have to put too much thought into it, and it goes with everything. Instead of getting into an all-black ensemble rut, though, add in some fun details by mixing in metallics. Throw on a silver bag or a gold patent belt, or simply polish your nails in a glittery hue.

winter wardrobe

One of my favorite things about dressing for winter is the variety of fabrics you can incorporate into one outfit. This strategy adds an important texture and breaks up the layers in a way that makes them seem intentional, instead of simply bulky. The three main things I focus on during the winter months are great sweaters, soft scarves, and unexpected patterns.

my favorite winter fabric/ textures

Lace (extra points if it's in a moody color like black)
Sequins
Mohair (in pale pastels)
Velvet
Satin
Wool
Cashmere
Leather
Silk chiffon
Tulle

I stock up on tissue-thin cashmere knits since they're a great base for layering (as shown here). They look and feel cozy, without relying on the weight of a massive fisherman's knit to provide warmth. I stick to mainly neutral colors (black, tan, white, and gray) and pick one fun shade per season to add a bit of variety.

Scarves are also a great way to not only stay warm, but also to add a pop of color to your face (I go for cherry reds and olive green). Switch up the way that you wear them so that you vary your look without much effort. I stick mainly with wool and silk-cashmere blends, as I find they hold their shape best.

Adding a bit of pattern to your winter wardrobe is essential to keeping ensembles from looking dull. I love plaid (see photo on the right), polka dots, stripes, and vibrant floral prints (keep the colors dark so they don't look too springlike), and when layered with basics, they'll make the entire outfit pop.

buying the perfect gift

It took me years to get behind the idea that holiday shopping should be done in advance. While it requires a lot of prep work, it will also ensure that your gifts are well thought out and that you won't spend hours looking for a parking space at the mall on Christmas Eve. Additionally, it means that you get to indulge in all the fun activities (baking cookies, watching nostalgic movies, going ice-skating) instead of stressing about a bunch of last-minute obligations. Here's how I tackle my holiday shopping, which I aim to finish by the first week in December.

Make a list. Write down a detailed inventory of people for whom you're going to get gifts. This should include everyone, even if you just plan to buy them small items (like a card with cash for your mailman or cookies for a neighbor).

Budget. Next to the person's name, come up with a general idea of what you'd like to spend. It doesn't have to be exact, but it will help you avoid looking at items that are too pricey.

Identify likes and hobbies. For those people who are notoriously tough to find the right gift for (hi, Dad!), start by taking notes on what they do like. For my dad, that list would look something like this: golfing, entertaining, reading, and music. Once you see the list, it will often spark ideas (like a new shirt for golf or a great platter for hors d'oeuvres).

Make a game plan. Once you have an idea of what you want to get people (this can be very general—like some sort of beauty product for a girlfriend), strategize on how to do it in the most efficient way. If you're going to the mall, have a shopping list so that you don't return home and then realize you forgot something. It might seem intense, but it will make the entire gift-giving process that much more enjoyable.

Wrap ahead. After all your gifts have been found, you might be tempted just to throw the bags and packages in a closet, but resist the urge and wrap them up immediately instead. Once they're wrapped (and labeled), you're done! You can sit back and relax while everyone else begins the frenzied rush to get everything finished before the holidays.

gift guide

Gifts should be personal and meaningful, but certain items are so great that they're universally accepted as making fabulous presents. Here are some of the ones that I love to give:

for guys

Tips: Think of things that every guy should own but might not necessarily splurge on for himself. Those everyday items can be made more special with engraved notes or monogrammed pieces.
Specifically: Money clip, keychain, wallet, belt, watch, book (cookbook from his favorite restaurant or a great chef, an artist he likes, or something based on a hobby), nice grooming products, a travel bag, some sort of subscription (to a video service like Netflix; a [fill in the blank] of the month, so that he receives beer/bacon/wine throughout the year; or his favorite magazine), a masculine-smelling candle, sunglasses, a nice bottle of alcohol, or some sort of electronics-related thing (a DVD, an iPad, a video game, or a new digital camera).

for girls

Tips: Girls like pretty things that aren't always as practical as those gifts given to guys, but instead are aesthetically pleasing and special.
Specifically: Stationery, jewelry, bath products, a gift certificate to something they love (to their favorite coffee shop or salon for a mani/pedi), a great beauty product, a bottle of champagne with two champagne flutes/coupes, items to hold little accessories (like pretty bowls, glasses, or trays), a framed picture, tickets to an upcoming concert, a soft scarf, a hair accessory, or an ordinary object that's been monogrammed (think napkins, coasters, etc.).

homemade gifts

Any gift that is well thought out is a sweet gesture, but there's something about making something yourself that adds an even more personal touch. Best of all, a lot of great gifts are easy to make and very affordable.

food/drink
Everyone loves to receive something from the kitchen. Figure out your specialty and wrap it up in a way that feels unique and appealing. Some of my favorite foods to give as gifts are homemade jams, cookies, breads, muffins, pastries, and caramel corn. Wrap them in simple packaging, like a basket with clear cellophane, and tie with a festive ribbon. You can also infuse your own alcohol (my favorite combination to make is Meyer lemon vodka). Wash lemons, slice them up, and put them into a large jar with a tightly fitting lid. Add vodka (the more distilled, the better), seal, and let soak for three to five days. Then just package it up with pretty bottles with labels and give them out as gifts.

music
A mix CD is one of my favorite gifts to give and receive. When someone takes the time to put together a great playlist, it's a nice way to be introduced to some of his or her favorite music. As with every gift, the packaging is also important, so add a personal note to the CD and label it.

photographs
One of the easiest gifts to give is a picture of you and the recipient in a pretty frame. Make sure the two go together, so that if it was a photograph taken at the beach, pair it with a simple and natural frame. If the picture is from a fancy wedding, gussy it up with a more glamorous frame that has some serious sparkle. On the back of the picture, write the place and date and a sweet note.

paper gratitude

Handwritten thank-you notes are one of the last gracious gestures in a primarily digital age. And while it's nice to receive appreciation via any medium (even text or e-mail), there's something about getting a letter in the mail that's truly special. Here are my tips for keeping the tradition alive and impressing people while you're at it.

choose special stationery

You don't have to splurge on embossed notecards or personalized stationery to make a statement. Instead, pick something that speaks to you. It can be as simple as getting some scalloped-edged cards and corresponding bright envelopes rather than a packaged set. I always like to keep two options on hand: one that feels a bit more formal and one that's playful and fun. This way, no matter the person or the gift they've given you, you'll be prepared to thank them in a way that's appropriate.

be timely

Though it's not always feasible, aim to send out a thank-you note within one to three days of receiving the gift. This way, it's top of mind, you'll get it off your plate, and you'll earn a gracious reputation.

keep it short

The thank-you notes I wrote as an adolescent were atrocious. They were long, unfocused, and I can only assume that they made the recipient regret giving me the gift in the first place. Now I stick to a very simple, yet straightforward format that makes writing notes painless and easy.

a sample thank-you note

Example: Aunt Rebecca gave me a pair of sunglasses for Christmas.

Dear Aunt Rebecca,

Thank you for my new sunglasses. They're absolutely beautiful and will come in very handy for our upcoming trip to Hawaii. It was great seeing you and Uncle Mike during the holidays, and I look forward to spending time with you this March. Thanks again for your gift.

Love,
Emily

The Format:
1. Address the person.
2. Express thanks for the specific gift ("my new sunglasses"). If you were given money, thank the person for the "generous gift." It sounds a lot less tacky than money/cash/dough. If you were given a gift certificate, make sure to mention the actual store ("thank you for the gift certificate to Anthropologie."). If someone hosted you for a weekend or for a lovely meal, simply thank him or her for the hospitality.
3. Describe how you intend to use the item. If you were given a new dress, say something like, "The dress is stunning, and it will be the perfect thing to wear for all of my holiday parties this season." If given money or a gift certificate, let them know what you intend to purchase. For example, "I can't wait to purchase the Annick Goutal perfume that I've been wanting for months!"
4. Mention time spent together and the next time you'll see each other.
5. Thank them again.
6. Sign off.

duly noted

There's nothing wrong with buying someone a card (whether it's for a birthday, expressing condolence, or as a congratulations), but if you have the time to make one yourself, it makes a big difference. Here are some of the things I always keep on hand so I can make my own personalized cards whenever one is needed.

tools

- Nice cardstock (I usually keep a few different colors on hand)
- Matching envelopes
- Stamps
- Hole punches
- Ribbon
- Glitter
- Glue stick
- Felt
- Tape (both Scotch and colored tape)
- Dried flowers
- Beads
- Good pens
- Wax seals + stamps

tied with a bow: gift wrapping 101

During the winter, it's good to keep a supply of gifts on hand for last-minute get-togethers (or unexpected guests). Things like bottles of wine, candles, or even pretty stationery make sweet gestures, but it's the packaging that will set them apart. I used to be that girl who would buy a great gift, only to present it to my friend still in its plastic bag. Not only did it feel incomplete, but the present itself didn't feel as special when not properly wrapped.

Some of my favorite wrapping supplies to keep on hand include pretty bags (that you can fill with homemade treats), raffia (to attach notes to bottles), ribbons, cards, a hole punch, metallic pens, and wrapping paper.

Here are some of my favorite ways to package gifts: rustic (with brown paper + raffia), bright (with floral wrapping paper + a tied-on brooch), whimsical (with starry paper + sparkly ribbon + rock candy), cheerful (with sunshine yellow paper + dried flowers), and festive (with brown paper + dried holly berries + a simple note).

beauty

Drab weather calls for fun
makeup and hair. Embrace
classic colors, like tomato red on
your fingernails, and don't
be afraid to add some glitter.
Tried-and-true favorites like
winged eyeliner with pink
lips look glamorous when set
against the snow.

5 winter beauty must-haves for any budget

1

Hair: smoothing serum (to help pretty hairstyles sleek). *Splurge*: Paul Mitchell's "Super Skinny Serum." *Steal*: Aussie's "Smoothing Serum."

2

Face: primer (to help your makeup stay put throughout entire parties). *Splurge*: Bare Minerals's "Prime Time." *Steal*: Rimmel's "Fix and Perfect."

3

Body: heavy moisturizer (for dull, flaky skin). *Splurge*: Bliss's "Energizing Cream." *Steal*: Aveeno's "Daily Moisturizing Lotion."

4

Lips: a deep, plum/wine lipstick (makes a big impact, with little effort). *Splurge*: Yves Saint Laurent's "Noir Laque." *Steal*: L'Oréal's "Spice."

5

Nails: a classic, bright red (never out of style, just keep your nails short and clean). *Splurge*: Chanel's "Dragon." *Steal*: Essie's "Fishnet Stockings."

* All Splurge items are shown on the left, Steal items on the right.

winterized beauty

With countless parties and events to attend during the winter months, it's important to change up not only your party attire, but also your beauty routine. Here are my three favorite looks that will be sure to make an impact.

updo (slightly disheveled) + red lips

The focus here should be on your lips, so pin up your hair in a style that's sophisticated but doesn't look too perfect. Let out a few pieces of hair by your face and keep the rest of your look really simple. A swipe of bronzer, a dab of highlighting cream on the apples of your cheeks, one coat of black mascara, and a bright red lip. See page 104 for more on how to wear bright lipstick.

bold smoky eye + light lip gloss

I always feel like the most sultry version of myself when my eyes are lined in smoky shadows (see above). Don't feel confined to just black and grays—explore jewel-tone shades like dark emerald and deep amethyst too. Since a smoky eye is really intense, a light-reflecting pink gloss is the ideal choice for your lips. See page 144 for more detailed instructions for how to achieve this look.

cat eye + pink lipstick

I love this look (see left). It feels wonderfully retro, but when paired with a sleek hairstyle and current clothes, it has modern appeal. Line your eyes with a dramatic sweep of liquid liner that flips up toward the ends for major impact. Pick a true pink lipstick that's equal parts Barbie and Brigitte Bardot. See page 146 for how to master winged eyeliner.

how to: smoky eye

Long before I had any clue about how to apply makeup properly, I found that a classic smoky eye was relatively easy to master. While the look may seem severe at first, it's a great way to add a dramatic touch to your nighttime beauty routine. The key is all in the balance and keeping the rest of your look simple and subdued.

tools

Eyeliner
Dark eye shadow
Highlighting cream in a
  pearly white
Eyelash curler
Mascara
Light pink/nude lip gloss

1 Line your inner eyes with eyeliner (kohl versions glide on easiest and stay put the longest), going over it a few times so the color is really pigmented.

2 With some eyeliner, trace the outside corners of your eye, on both the top and bottom (don't worry about it looking perfect; it's supposed to look a little messy).

3 Add dark eye shadow to the top lid (I usually use black and then blend it well so that it gets gradually lighter the higher it goes on the eyelid).

4 Dab your highlighting cream onto the inner corners of your eyes, along the brow bone, and down the bridge of the nose.

5 Curl your lashes and add two coats of mascara, and then apply the lip gloss.

how to: winged eyeliner

I love the look of dramatic winged eyeliner—it manages to make your eyes look both seductive and sweet at the same time. Liquid liner is notoriously difficult to work with, since it smears easily and you have to have a steady hand to make it look good. Here are my tips for applying it.

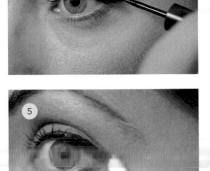

tools

Eyelash curler
Mascara
Liquid eyeliner
Cotton swab

1 Curl your lashes and apply mascara.

2 Using liquid eyeliner, make tiny dots in between individual lashes on your upper lid. Then connect them so there's one very fine line.

3 With your elbow propped on a steady surface (this will help you create a straighter line), line the top of your lashes, making the line slightly thicker as you get closer to the outside of the eye.

4 Use the upward curve of your lower lash line as a guide for making the angle at the end of the line you are drawing. Keeping a light touch, extend the line upward and flick at the end to create a tapered finish.

5 Use a swab to clean up any smudges or to thin out the eyeliner. This is a polished look, so it should be very precise.

at home

Decorating your place during the winter can be challenging. You want it to feel festive, with subtle nods to the holidays that are both cozy and inviting. In searching for that ideal balance, I've figured out simple tricks (from finding the right art on a budget to decorating for the season) that make a big impact.

a cool habitat

There are little things you can do at home that tune in to the season. One of the simplest ways to make a place feel a bit more winter-appropriate is by putting up a bare-branched wreath. It's a decoration that brings nature indoors (or right outside your door) and is reminiscent of the weather. And it's kind of like a blank canvas, which I much prefer over something that feels too holiday-esque or crafty. I like wreaths made of twigs that let you dress them up whatever way works for you. Either spray-paint miniature pinecones and tie them on with string, attach fallen leaves, or hang miniature silver balls to give it a glamorous touch.

I also like quick changes that make a big impact. I hang outerwear in a visible spot so going outside is easy and make the bed inviting by setting up my heated mattress pad and getting out the flannel sheets. I go with darker, richer hues everywhere—changing the towels in the bathroom and kitchen is one good way to do this. If you have a mantel or a (nonworking) fireplace, fill it with wood, candles, acorns, pinecones, or pumpkins. Even if you don't have a fireplace, you can simply throw some wood into a basket or bucket to create a homey vibe.

baby, it's cold outside— cozy essentials

- woodsy scented candles
- extra blankets
- dark, moody flowers
- bowls of things to munch on (like nuts and candies)
- firewood
- ingredients for warm drinks (like hot chocolate, hot toddies, or apple cider)

the power of paint

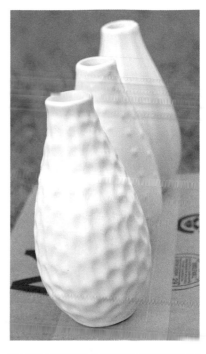

One of the simplest ways to update your place is to use paint. Spray paint requires very little prep work or additional tools (no paintbrushes necessary!) and comes in a wide variety of colors. I always keep a few cans on hand in neutrals like gold, black, and white so that I can spruce things up within a few minutes. Here are some of the ways I've used paint to add a bit of polish around my place.

small objects

Do you have a set of mismatched candlesticks or porcelain vases that have lost their luster? A quick coat of paint will bring them back to life. Items to consider: small vases, candlesticks, bookends, figurines, frames, etc.

furniture

The quickest way to transform a worn piece of furniture is with a fresh coat of paint. My dark, drab nightstands were immediately freshened up with white paint (if it's wood, just make sure to sand and add a coat of primer before you begin). Items to consider: mirrors, side tables, benches, chairs, etc.

picasso for pennies—finding art on a budget

My decor has evolved over time, as I think all things should. My first apartment, straight out of college, had a very shabby chic vibe, since I furnished it all from flea markets (I now like to mix and match vintage pieces with things that are more modern). I didn't have the funds to buy new expensive art, but I had grown out of the posters I taped to my wall when I was in college. I quickly learned that with a little creativity, I could add artistic touches without breaking the bank.

think beyond framed art
In my office, I've hung a large, sparkly garland (see opposite) made of different fabrics from one wall to the other in lieu of filling the space with smaller pieces. It makes a big impact, adds a playful element to the room, and helps the entire space feel complete.

frame things other than "art"
Many things that aren't typically seen as art are beautiful and interesting. This might be a love letter that your great-grandfather sent to your great-grandmother, a cool menu, a birthday card you wrote when you were five, or even an intricate piece of wallpaper. An elegant frame ties it all together and usually the more

sentimental something it is, the more it really resonates.

incorporate what you love
Whether it's your collection of old vinyl records or a bunch of different-sized mirrors, display your favorite things. It's a fun way to express your style in an artistic way.

frame favorite quotes/lyrics
Write them out yourself with a paintbrush or pick a great font on the computer and make a printout. Stay away from the more obvious/overused lines ("Let It Be" and "All You Need Is Love" come to mind) and think of lyrics that mean something to you. My favorite lyric is from a Bob Dylan

song, which is "Last night I danced with a stranger. But she just reminded me you were the one." It might not resonate with everyone, but since it spoke to me, I framed that quote and hung it in my office.

create art
You don't have to be an artist to make a great painting. Get a canvas, buy some paints, and experiment a bit. Mimicking modern art, which often has canvases painted with one bold color and a couple of paint splatters, is fairly simple. Once framed, your piece will look much more refined and polished.

framed walls

A few years back, I started collecting vintage frames from the flea market. They were mismatched and all different varnishes, but I found their intricacies too pretty to pass up. Since I never got around to filling them with pictures or mirrors the way I had initially intended, I decided to use them as art. When painted the same color as the wall, they add great dimension and can be hung over a nightstand, down a long hallway, or even in lieu of a headboard. I painted mine the same gray as my bedroom walls (Benjamin Moore's "Pelican Gray"), and I love the subtle effect they bring to the room.

1 Pick up frames at the market—the more intricate, the better. Sometimes you have to overlook bad paint or ugly artwork (remember, you can just remove that). Pay attention to the detailing. That's what will really stand out on your wall.

2 Prep the frames. Give them a good dusting and remember that wood frames may need some sanding before you begin. Brush on one to two coats of paint (depending on the color).

3 Once you have painted them all the same color, let them dry completely.

4 Make a game plan. Before you start nailing things to the wall, get a general idea of what the layout will be. Measure the area and map it out on your floor using painter's tape as a guide. From there, play around with different pairings—for instance, one large frame next to two smaller ones, with a rectangular frame below one that's circular.

5 Find the right wall, a blank space that could use some texture. Hang all the frames and secure them properly.

food and entertaining

When it's cold out, there's nothing more appealing than classic comfort food. I find myself making soups and baking cookies on a weekly basis, both for the enjoyment and to make sure my place always smells and feels like home.

I like to keep winter gatherings at my place über casual and easy. I enjoy inviting people over for a quick glass of (spiked) eggnog or to help frost cookies (you can see my guide on how to make them on pages 77–78). It reminds people that despite everything they have going on, it's nice to take time for the season's simplest pleasures.

oscar party

I'm indifferent to the Super Bowl, so the Academy Awards is the televised event of the year that I look forward to the most. It's the perfect excuse to throw a party, hang out with your girlfriends, swoon over all the dresses, and eat delicious treats.

the breakdown

A lot of people are intimidated by the idea of hosting a party. When you break it down, though, it can be really simple and fun. Here are the three things I took into account when throwing my Oscar Party:

- **Pick a theme.** Think of colors you want to incorporate (I chose red and gold) and use those as a guide while you're planning your party.

- **Have a dress code.** I had friends come over in casual clothes, but with glamorous, over-the-top jewelry and bright lipstick. That way, people were comfortable, but felt a little more elegant and playful than usual.

- **Have snacks.** Obviously people like to have good food at parties, but also make sure the snacks are easy to eat (one-bite things that don't require forks and knives) and remind people of being at the movies. Stock up on things like popcorn and classic candies and package them with a simple ribbon or in a cute baggie to make them even more appealing.

details

Pay attention to the little things that will make your gathering feel extra special, such as:

- old-school popcorn bags
- customized candy bags
- striped straws for champagne
- themed desserts (star cookies and black-tie cupcakes)
- red and white polka-dot napkins with star confetti

general entertaining must-dos

plan ahead
It's crucial that you be prepared so that, on the day of your party, everything is pretty much already done. Buy prepackaged snacks ahead of time, make desserts and store them as needed, buy beverages, and double-check that you have everything you might need to serve them (ice, napkins, etc.).

make people feel at home
You don't need a gigantic sectional sofa to ensure that your guests are comfortable, but make sure everyone can see the television, has something to sit on (whether it's a pillow on the floor or an extra chair), and always has a drink in hand.

create a nice atmosphere
Have fresh flowers in the house. Light a candle in the bathroom. Make sure lights are dimmed to set the mood, but make sure they're not so dark that your guests can't see.

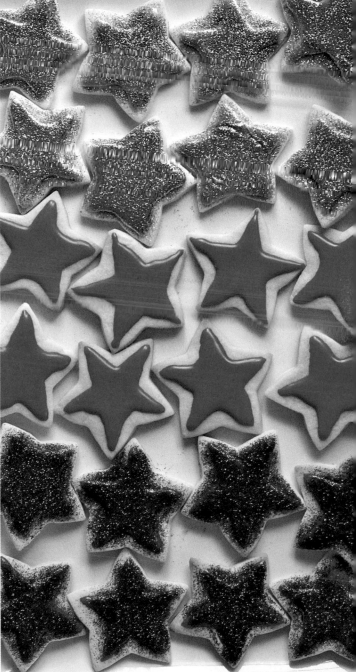

table manners

More often than not, I remember a well-set table more than the actual food at a dinner party. It creates such a nice ambience and really sets the stage for a great evening. Here are some of the traditional rules I follow, and a few of the tips to keep it feeling fresh and fun.

layer
Instead of just throwing plates down on the table, add different layered elements to make the overall effect appealing and intricate. During the holidays, for instance, I like using basic burlap as a runner (it adds such a rustic vibe). Then I add other fabrics like tulle or taffeta on top for more of a festive touch.

place settings
The holidays are a great time to make a table feel glamorous and to make the most out of each meal. Even on nights when we're not hosting (and possibly just eating takeout), it makes a big difference when the table's set and candles are lit. I like to keep place mats and napkins simple, with muted colors and metallic accents. Buy some metallic fabrics at a local craft store and use them to tie napkins or layer them on top of the place mat.

A general rule of thumb to remember when putting out the place settings for a casual meal is that the silverware that you use first should be placed farthest from the plate. So on the left side of the plate, you should first have a salad fork, then the regular fork. To the right of the plate, you should have a knife (make sure to put out a steak knife if you're serving meat), followed by a teaspoon. Either fold the napkin and lay it on top of the plate or use a napkin ring and position it horizontally above the plate. Set both a water glass and wineglass to the right of the plate—drinks should always be on the right. A quick (though somewhat embarrassing) way to remember which side the drinks should be on is to make a lowercase b and d with your hands; the one that looks like a d is on the right, which is where your drink should be!

final touches
Once the table's set, I like to add flowers, candles, and a pretty salt and pepper set. And instead of bringing a water filter pitcher to the table, I like to pour water into glass bottles for a more chic presentation.

cupcake 101

I consider myself quite the cupcake connoisseur and fell in love with the bite-sized confections long before they ever gained notoriety. They're the perfect choice for a birthday, a party, or just because, and there really is an art to making the perfect cupcake. Here are my simple tips.

- **Use a box.** This goes against one of my core beliefs that in the kitchen homemade is always best. The few times I attempted to make homemade cupcakes, they tasted like dry cornbread. Instead, buy a cake mix (I always keep one yellow and one chocolate on hand) and simply follow the instructions for making cupcakes (or a full-sized cake). To make sure that all of the cupcakes come out the same size, use a small ice cream scoop to help with consistency.

- **Make homemade frosting.** While using a box mix is fine for the cupcakes themselves, it's important to make your own frosting. If you do this step, I can pretty much guarantee that nobody will know the difference.

- **Take your time on the frosting.** This is what people notice first (that, and cute cupcake liners), so try to make sure all your cupcakes are consistent. Don't be afraid to add elements like sprinkles, colored sugar, or candies, but I think the notion that "less is more" holds true in this case.

buttercream frosting

A classic buttercream frosting is one of the simplest recipes to make. It's deceptively light (it is called buttercroam, after all), fluffy, shiny, and incredibly versatile. The only thing that requires advance planning is that you need room-temperature butter—throwing it in the microwave won't work.

ingredients

Makes enough to frost 18 cupcakes

- 1 cup (2 sticks) butter
- 3 cups confectioners' sugar
- 1 teaspoon vanilla extract
- 3 to 5 drops food coloring (optional)

1   In a stand mixer fitted with the whisk attachment (or in a large bowl with a handheld mixer), beat the butter on high for 1 ½ minutes. Reduce the speed to low and begin adding the confectioners' sugar, 1 cup at a time. Once you're sure sugar won't fly everywhere, turn the mixer up to high speed. Beat until all the sugar has been added and is well incorporated.

2   Add the vanilla extract and food coloring, if you're using it, and beat for 2 more minutes, until the frosting is light and fluffy but still holds its shape.

frosting cupcakes

(Partially) homemade cupcakes are my favorite—they've been made with love, and any little imperfections simply make them more appealing. That being said, I do use a few frosting techniques to make them look more bakery than bake sale disaster.

tools

Pastry tip
Piping bag (or a Ziploc bag with one corner cut off)
1 batch Buttercream Frosting (page 161)
Freshly baked, cooled cupcakes
Additional toppings (sprinkles, colored sugar, etc.)

1 Choose your design. Pick a pastry tip that lends itself to the design you're going for. I usually stick to a classic swirl as in the design pictured here, so my two favorite tips are the large round and the medium-sized star.

2 Prep your piping bag. Once your frosting is ready, put it into a pastry bag (or plastic bag) that's been fitted with a tip. To do this, I like to rest the bag in a glass and fold the top out over the sides to hold it open, so that I don't make too much of a mess as I put the frosting in. Then, fold the bag back up and press the frosting down toward the tip, eliminating air bubbles as you go. Fold the top of the bag down (or zip up the plastic bag) so that once you start piping, the frosting doesn't come out the top.

3 Start icing. The key is to move in a slow, steady circle above the cupcake, holding the bag perfectly vertical. Apply even pressure by squeezing the bag with one hand and guiding it with the other. Start on the outer edge of the cupcake and make an even circle around the entire thing (make sure that you go all the way to the sides).

4 Create circles. After you've created the outside, start to make another circle by bringing the pastry tip inside and continue the same motion. Once you're done frosting and your tip is hovering over the middle of the cupcake, release pressure on the bag first, then lift it up with a straight motion.

details

I think that a perfectly frosted cupcake speaks for itself, but a light sprinkling of sanding sugar or a well-placed single candy can be an excellent way to finish.

icing on the cake

Knowing how to properly frost a cake is one of those useful skills that comes in handy more often than you'd think. The key is creating what's called a "crumb coat"—this is a thin layer of frosting that helps seal in any crumbs before the final frosting layer is applied.

tools

Serrated knife or thin wire
2 freshly baked, cooled 9-inch round cakes
Baking sheet
Wax paper
Spoon
2 batches Buttercream Frosting (page 161)
Offset spatula
Sanding sugar
Pencil

1 Using the serrated knife or the wire, level the cakes, removing just the rounded tops to create an even surface. This step isn't necessary, but makes for a more professional-looking final product.

2 Place both cakes on top of a baking sheet lined with wax paper. Dollop a good amount of frosting (start with about ½ cup) on top of each cake, making sure not to let the spoon touch the cake (you don't want crumbs in your frosting).

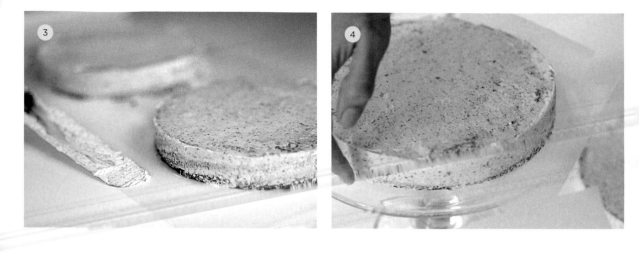

3   Using the offset spatula, slowly work your way around the cakes, smoothing out the sides and sealing in the crumbs. This layer of frosting should be very thin (nearly transparent) and even. Place the cakes, still on the baking sheet, into the fridge for 30 minutes to set.

4   Transfer the first layer of the cake onto a pedestal or cake stand. Tear off several large strips of wax paper and gently slip them under the cake. This will help keep the surface clean while you're frosting.

5   Frost the top of the cake, creating a thick, even layer (don't worry about the sides yet).

6   Gently place the other layer on top, making sure both cakes are lined up.

7   Continue frosting, first covering the top and then spreading frosting along the sides of the cake. Use gentle sweeping motions to smooth the surface of the cake.

8   As an extra decorating element, I like to add a thin layer of sanding sugar to the top of the cake. To do this, with a pencil trace a circle on a piece of wax paper that's a few inches smaller in diameter than the cake (I use a plate for this) and cut it out.

9   Lightly place the circular piece of wax paper in the middle of the cake. Sprinkle the sanding sugar so that it falls just along the outer rim of the top of the cake.

10 Carefully peel away the wax paper and smooth the surface again with the offset spatula.

blue ombré layer cake

For a fun variation on a typical cake, I make each layer a different color, so that once you cut the cake, the inside makes a big impact. I like to do an ombré effect (a gradual changing of shades all the same general color) by using varying blue hues inside and covering the outside with white frosting— a perfect wintery color combination.

To do this, simply make enough batter for a couple extra cake layers. Divide the batter into separate bowls and, using a single bottle of food coloring, add varying amounts to each bowl. For example, bowl #1—no food coloring, bowl #2—two drops, bowl #3—three drops, and so on. Bake each layer separately, and once they've cooled, make sure to stack them according to their color intensity as you frost (see the instructions on page 165).

crash course on cheese

If I could eat only one thing for the rest of my life, I would undoubtedly pick cheese. When I was young, my dad would take me to a little cheese shop in downtown Mill Valley. You could smell it from several blocks away, and I was in love with the pungent, spicy smells inside. The store's owner would give me samples of cheeses from all over the world, served up on thin slices of baguette.

Since then, my love for cheese has only grown, which is why I've researched how to make the perfect cheese plate. The tiny shop in Mill Valley closed years ago, but I spent some time speaking with Raphael at the Beverly Hills Cheese Store to find out all the most important details. Whether you're serving it for a crowd or simply to enjoy on your own, here are my tips to ensure that your cheese plate is executed flawlessly.

Know the sources.
Once you've narrowed down the exact type of cheese you like, it will make picking out the right ones much less intimidating, so we'll start there. Here are the main types of milk used:

Goat: tangy, nutty, and a little barnyard-esque (this is because goats eat everything, so the flavors are really intricate). Pairs well with crisp white wines like Chardonnay or Chablis. Avoid pairing with red wine since the acidity in goat cheese will overwhelm the taste of the wine.

Sheep: creamy, slightly nutty, with a buttery finish. Pairs well with lighter reds, like Pinot Noirs or Tempranillos.

Cow: far and away the largest category of cheeses, so it's impossible to pinpoint the flavors since they range so greatly (from Brie to cheddar to Parmesan).

2 **Pay attention to texture.**
There are three main textures of cheeses:

Soft: easily spreadable, melts easily (example: Brie).

Semisoft: still quite soft, but with a firmer texture, that can be sliced (example: Gouda).

Hard: sliceable cheese that's dense and usually has been aged (example: cheddar).

3 **Choose your cheeses.**
A cheese plate should consist of a variety of cheeses. As a rule of thumb, you should include different types and textures: soft, semisoft, aged; mild, sharp, and blue. Take the majority of the cheeses out of the fridge about an hour before serving, so they have time to come to room temperature. Here are some excellent varieties to include:

Triple cream (soft, usually cow)
This cheese has a butterfat content higher than any other cheese, which is what makes it so dense and creamy.
Tip: Use a small serrated knife with holes to make it easier to slice.
Favorites: Saint Angel, Saint-André, Brillat-Savarin

Cheddar (aged, cow)
Cheddar is one of my favorite types of cheese—it's flavorful, packs a punch, and I think the

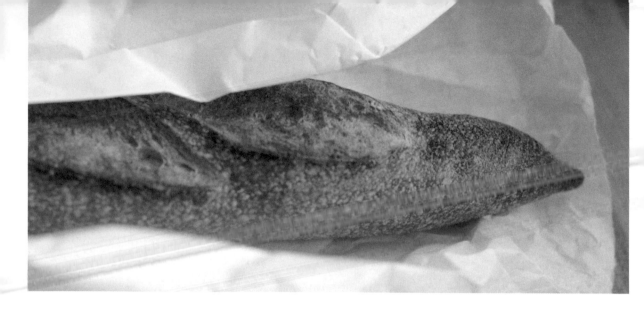

sharper it is, the better.
Tip: To get the best cheddar, pick ones that have been aged at least six years.
Favorites: Cabot, Old Quebec Vintage Cheddar, Fiscalini Aged Cheddar

Sheep's milk cheese (semisoft)

These cheeses are mild in flavor, but well-rounded.
Tip: Add some quince paste to really bring out the flavors of the cheese.
Favorites: Istara, Petit Basque, Manchego

Gouda (hard, goat)

A goat's milk gouda is a great cheese for beginners. It's smooth and velvety, and not too tangy.
Tip: Serve it with pear paste or sliced pears.
Favorites: Beemster, Arina, Cablanca

Blue (soft, cow)

Blue cheese can certainly be overpowering due to its pungent flavor, but if you stick to creamy varieties (versus those that are crumbly), the flavors are much less intense.
Tip: Make sure to end your cheese tasting with blue (never start with it), so that it doesn't warp your palette for the other cheeses.
Favorites: Saint Agur, Montbriac, Roquefort

4 Present your selection.

Now that you've chosen the cheeses to include on your plate, make sure they're presented in a way that's aesthetically pleasing and functional. I like to label my cheeses (either use a piece of slate that you can write on with chalk as a cheese board or simply include paper labels on the platter) so that people know what they're getting. Feel free to add little accoutrements, like sprigs of rosemary, a little honeycomb, fresh or dried fruit, quince paste, or nuts. Not only do they enhance the flavors, but also they make the overall presentation that much more appealing.

popping the cork

I always keep a bottle of champagne or sparkling wine chilling in the fridge. Not only is it great to have for unexpected guests, but it's also a nice reminder that little things also deserve celebrating.

Popping a bottle of champagne can be intimidating—I was convinced I was going to lose an eye the first time I tried on my own. The truth is, though, it's really simple once you know the steps (and precautions to take).

1 Remove champagne from fridge, after chilling for about 3 hours (or for a half hour in an ice bucket).

2 Peel off wrapper around cork, and then twist the wire ring to loosen and remove the wire cage around the cork.

3 Cover the top of the bottle with a clean dish towel.

4 Stand over a sink if possible and point the champagne bottle away from yourself (and anyone else).

5 Slowly start to twist the towel and cork underneath it while very gradually pulling outward. Once you hear the pop, wait a few seconds, then remove the towel.

6 Pour while holding the bottle at a slight diagonal against the inside rim of the glass.

winter cocktail: champagne cocktail

Since people are in festive spirits during the holidays, it's good to match their mood with an equally fun drink. Champagne cocktails are classic for a reason—they're crisp and refreshing, and a little bubbly goes a long way.

ingredients

Makes 1 cocktail

- 1 sugar cube
- 2 to 3 dashes Angostura bitters
- Champagne
- 1 maraschino cherry and/or an orange peel

Place the sugar cube in the bottom of a champagne glass and splash it with bitters. Fill the glass with champagne. Garnish with a cherry or an orange peel.

Tipsy Tip: Invest in a few vintage champagne coupes—they make even the simplest drinks (like this cocktail) seem infinitely more festive.

resources

Here's a collection of a few of my favorite websites—many of which also have fantastic stores that are great places to browse, if one is in your area. You've seen a lot of their products on my blog and in this book, and this list is only a starting point when you're looking for something fresh and fun, for either your wardrobe or home.

style

www.net-a-porter.com
My go-to for splurges, whether it's a new dress, a fantastic pair of shoes, or an of-the-moment bag.

www.pixiemarket.com
Loaded with pieces that you don't see anywhere else. Expect bright colors, unexpected cuts, and unique jewelry.

www.shopbop.com
Not only is shopbop home to tons of fabulous designers (both established and up-and-coming), they offer great customer service with free two-day shipping and returns.

www.jcrew.com
My closet is filled with J. Crew classics. Their outerwear (like blazers, coats, and sweaters) is worth the investment and their bright basics are a great addition to anyone's wardrobe.

www.zara.com
This is the best spot for on-trend pieces that look like they're fresh off the runway (without the price tag).

beauty

www.bluemercury.com
A site/store that carries the best in luxury beauty products (favorites include: Diptyque candles, Molton Brown hand wash, and Oribe hair products).

www.sephora.com
A wide selection of the best beauty brands with a great return policy (plus you get to pick three samples with each order).

www.drugstore.com
The affordable brands found at your local drugstore with the convenience of not having to leave home.

at home

www.westelm.com
Modern home furnishing that are both sleek and sophisticated (I especially love their accessories—like their trays, mirrors, and rugs).

www.jaysonhome.com
This site is like shopping at a Parisian flea market that's stocked with only the most unique pieces.

www.shopterrain.com
One of my favorite sites for beautiful home goods (like rustic coasters, vintage-inspired glassware, and high quality linens) that also make for perfect gifts.

www.thecontainerstore.com
I stock up on plastic containers, storage bins, thin fabric hangers, and pretty much anything else that will help me stay organized.

www.aplusrstore.com
The most expertly edited site filled with cool serving pieces, quirky accessories, and decorative objects to make your space feel chic.

www.anthropologie.com
The best place for picking up patterned bowls, pretty trays, and serving pieces that will make your kitchen a lot more stylish.

food and entertaining

www.confectioneryhouse.com
A wonderfully curated site stocked with every sort of baking supply you'll ever need. I load up on sprinkles, unique baking cups, seasonal treats, and cute packaging.

www.surlatable.com
This one-stop-shop is home to a large variety of kitchen supplies, including cookware, cutlery, and electronics.

acknowledgments

The past year and a half I spent working on this book (while maintaining my blog, collaborating on several partnerships, and planning my wedding) has been a lesson in finding balance. The days were long, but inspired, and it was such a thrill to bring my blog to life in the form of a book. None of it could have happened if not for several very important people.

First and foremost, I'd like to acknowledge my husband, Geoffrey, for his unwavering support, love, and encouragement. Thank you for believing in me when I didn't and for making each day better than the last.

To my parents, who have always inspired me to work hard and to pursue what makes me happy. Dad, thank you for being my biggest fan and for taking each one of my calls with more enthusiasm than I deserve. Mom, thank you for your steadfast interest in all that matters to me and for showing me unconditional love.

To my editors, Laura and Rebecca, please accept my sincere gratitude for your continued patience and faith in my work. To Seth and Roy, for translating my vision into beautifully designed pages. To my literary agent, Ryan, who first insisted I write a book (to which I initially responded with laughter). To X, thank you for reading and rereading my drafts with such enthusiasm. To Eden, Rachel, and Tal—thank you for being the kind of friends I aspire to be.

Finally, I'd like to thank the readers of my blog for making my work such a pleasure to share. Your excitement and encouragement moves me daily and I am so appreciative of all of your support.

ALLEGRA HICKS

AVEDON FASHION

BAZAAR GREATEST HITS